BLOWING AWAY THE COBWEBS
THE NATURE OF ANGUS

Margaret Mitchell and Alison Hamilton

First published in 2014 by agetus
Email: agetus@btinternet.com

ISBN 978-0-9928669-0-7

Typeset in Garamond 13pt

Printed and Bound by Robertsons Printers, Forfar, Scotland

Front cover: Lunan Bay
Back cover :   Blue Hole Agate © National Museums Scotland

This book is for our Angus families in remembrance of them.

CONTENTS

Contents continued   Page No.

List of Maps and Photographs
Bibliography and References

The four stories marked with an asterix * have previously appeared in The Countryman magazine

ACKNOWLEDGEMENTS

Our thanks go to the following:

Angus Archives, Forfar
Angus Council
Brown, Son & Ferguson Ltd, Printers and Publishers,
    Glasgow
Liverpool Public Library
Museums of Kirriemuir and Montrose
National Archives of Scotland, Edinburgh
National Library of Scotland, Edinburgh (Maps Collection)
Royal Commission on the Ancient and Historical
    Monuments of Scotland
RSPB
Scottish Archive Network
Scottish Wildlife Trust
Signal Tower Museum, Arbroath
St Andrews University, St Andrews, Fife – Department of
    Collections
The Collections Unit, Leisure & Culture, Dundee
The Newspaper Licensing Agency Ltd
The Picture Library, National Museums Scotland,
    Edinburgh

Our thanks to Arbroath Herald Newspaper; to Norman Atkinson of Angus Council Cultural Services for his kind permission to use a photograph of The Reliance bale of canvas; to Brown, Son & Ferguson Ltd, Glasgow for their kind permission to use their photograph of Flying Horse figurehead; National Museums Scotland Picture Library for their photographs of agates; the National Library of Scotland for their permission to reproduce maps relating to

Springfield, Arbroath and the staff of Arbroath, Forfar and Kirriemuir Libraries. We also thank Aileen Rogers for her enthusiasm and encouragement. Thanks also to Dave Barber for all his help.

Every effort has been made by the authors to obtain permission from copyright holders but if any credits have been omitted, please accept our apologies.

INTRODUCTION

Angus lies in the shadow of some of the larger counties in Scotland. Geographically the city of Dundee is in Angus but unfortunately it has ring-fenced itself and created an area calling itself 'Tayside'. Angus has lost its heart and has become fragmented. Many local towns and villages are feeling empty and the lack of tourists supports this.

Nan Shepherd, climber and nature writer, once said "I only write when I feel that there is something that simply must be written." This book has been written on the back of that. Nature writing has been on the whole neglected and that is unforgiveable for Angus, with its ancient landscape, has much to offer. Experiencing the natural world should be part of our everyday lives, not just a hobby we 'do' at weekends.

Wildlife is on our doorstep. Even a tiny garden will give a continuity of life and give us a look into the living creatures' world and their universe. We should lament the passing of a species of wildflower, a bird, insect or animal if it is no more for we cannot resurrect that which has gone.

We must care for our magical places for this makes us who we are.

Angus County has been our inspiration. We live in its countryside and regularly visit its coast line. It is unfailing in its simplistic means to please for 'there is beauty in everything but everyone does not see it.'

We hope you enjoy our nature rambles with a little bit of history thrown in.

PART ONE

SALTY AIR

A VIEW FROM THE SHORE

The tide is coming in and the white waves dance as they push their way over the rocks shallow beneath the water close to the beach.

The life boat passes bobbing up and down. It is on an exercise forever watchful at this time of year for it is early winter and the sea can change from mild to tempest very quickly.

There is a fair wind today and the sky is grey. The water looks cold and uninviting.

I can just make out the Bell Rock lighthouse, standing as a proud sentinel built on sea rocks eleven miles from land, a saviour to many over the years. My gaze follows a herring gull as it interrupts my view, so graceful the wings barely moving, just enough to navigate direction. It soars on a draught of wind and flies out over the sea. It is many years since these gulls have followed the herring boats. It may look as if these birds are doing well but unbelievably, the herring gull is on the 'red' list of the RSPB along with the common gull on 'amber'. This smaller gull with its yellow beak and yellow legs once so plentiful now thinly scattered along our shore; I count it a good day when I see one.

The shore is forever changing. When the tide returns, it is never to quite the same spot. It is an ancient place as it was here that life, as we know it, all began. But the quiet meeting place of land and sea of old is now charged with fury and what took thousand of years to alter our shore is now happening in decades. The bowels of the earth, the sea floor, and the glaciers are all in competition and the sea is never still.

Nature is unsympathetic to the weak and takes no prisoners. The creatures and birds of the beach of today are the champions of a long line of foot soldiers. Watching a herring gull in flight, soaring sky-ward with such grace and beauty, carried by the wind, it manoeuvres and feels the salt breeze within its feathers. It lands with ease on rocks, beach or sea for it has taken millions of years of evolution to create this ultimate flying machine of the sea shore and child of the wind.

Birds have a tip-top air conditioning system. They need to for flying requires great effort. Their breathing is fast and their heart beats many times per second, its red cells outweigh the white. Birds prepare their food in their 'crop' prior to entering the stomach where the elastic fibres are capable of contracting and relaxing to produce bodily movement, giving them the strength and physical power to feed their young many many times a day.

Something has disturbed the sanderlings. A group of them rise and fly up the beach. They are in their winter plumage, pale grey and white underneath; wonderful to watch as they run after the retreating wave, their little bills searching the sand and, just as the next wave returns to this marginal world, the sanderlings run up the beach on their thin little legs as fast as they can go. As if in unison, they all dart down again and so it goes on. Their frantic winter feeding is necessary to build up their reserves for the flight to the breeding grounds in early summer. They return to the Arctic Tundra, the young hide in the blossom of the tundra flowers. The bird is in its breeding plumage, brown with variegated spots of shading. Hopefully they return to us late August, early September.

Although cold today unlike yesterday, it has begun much brighter, the grey sky has gone and the high cirrus clouds have an ethereal look. This cloud holds ice crystals and is the birthplace of snow. The herring gull greets me with its head thrown back and is in full voice. Others join in and then all is quiet. They await the return of the sea. Their white heads, black tipped wings, yellow beak with red markings and legs pale red seem to glow today in the cold air.

The black headed gulls so called because of their summer plumage begin to squabble over a tiny morsel; a mock fight starts but ends as a redshank lands close by. It stands like a soldier on guard, missing nothing. Suddenly the flash of the probing beak and a small mollusc has become breakfast. The legs are fairly long as befits a wader and there can be no mistaking those bright red legs. A flock of black headed gulls have settled on the beach and are paddling at the edge, allowing the tide to cover their feet. Being winter, their heads are white with a dark mark above their eye. Although their numbers appear to be strong here in Angus, this bird is also on amber alert.

There are several tide lines on the beach, some higher, others lower. Levels vary daily on the wish of the moon and sun. The moon, our closest neighbour, pulls at the earth and in so doing affects the seas and oceans. 'Spring tides' come twice a month at a new moon and the full moon. The tide is high at these times and leaves its mark high on the beach and, in turn, the retreat of the sea 'ebb tide' goes further out than usual. The 'neap tide' is when the high water level reaches its lowest point and the seaweed line on the beach is quite far down. These small tides are at half moon periods, several days after a new moon and several days after a full moon.

I cannot see him but I hear the call of the redshank somewhere on the rocks, a loud cry of 'teuk teuk teuk'. The oyster catchers fly over, noisy as usual. There must be 20 or 30 of them although both male and female look alike. There can be no mistaken identity with this bird; long orange/red beak, longish red legs and body black and white. They have come to rest on a group of rocks which the tide will cover soon but they have folded their wings with heads tucked in and are balancing remarkably on one leg and have gone to sleep.

A shag flies into view, inches from the water on the look-out for a fish shoal. He is a wonderful swimmer and will dive great depths for his meals. At 30 inches or so in length, he is one of our largest sea birds, only the cormorant and the heron are slightly larger.

There is little growing vegetation along this shore as fierce winds and seas tear everything up. Only patches of marram grass survive, tough as old boots, a coarse sea-straw that can cut the bare legs of the unwary.

A bright orange 'sunk' (lobster/crab pot) lies broken on the beach. Last night's rough sea had no doubt wrenched it from its mooring approximately half a mile out. One less for the fisherman to haul on to his small boat but a replacement will be quickly made and put down next tide.

A fog is rolling in from the horizon with an eerie silence. The low flying vapour of moist salt air has reduced my visibility. A shiver runs through me. It is time to turn for home. I hear the foghorn and wish all at sea a safe passage.

Artist unknown

Gulls in silhouette

ROCK POOLS

Rock pools are magical places, each pool different from the last, never knowing what the sea had left behind; living creatures who must survive until the next tide; tiny microscopic diatoms drifting gently on the surface of the pool. Looking into the water, you feel its ageless appeal. You learn early on when examining pools to be very gentle so as not to disturb the inhabitants and that the visibility of clear water diminishes with eager disturbance.

The pebbles in the pool, so modest and unassuming are the product of ancient rocks, glacier driven, pounded and tumbled by the sea into works of art. Pebbles have been used for thousands of years for various things; tools, buildings, mosaics even jewellery but, in some countries, they have a spiritual meaning. In Japan, they are thought to be the secret hiding places of the gods so we are in good company!

The seaweed weaves and shimmers in the still water, some sunbathing on the beach and rocks. These are the plants of the sea but their surroundings make them different from the garden or wild flower varieties. There is no soil for them, they must gain a foothold on rocks or hold tightly on to a neighbouring plant. Where rain and prolonged dampness can aid or kill a land plant, it makes little difference to our marine organisms.

There are many species of seaweed but all are not present in our rock pool. For some, it is too cold and they require a warmer climate and much more light.

Artists and photographers particularly go on and on about light and their images of the seascapes can be breathtakingly beautiful in hues of blue and turquoise. The different colours within the light are absorbed at different levels of the sea and it diminishes at depth, where seaweed as we know it does not grow but this is about 200 feet. Our rock pool is a mere six to eight inches deep but sometimes, after a few wild and stormy tides, bits and pieces will have been deposited in the shallow pools having been torn from deeper moorings.

Sea water is generally a little alkaline (from an Arab word meaning charred ashes) being obtained from the ashes of certain green plants. Looking at our rock pool, if it has a lot of green algae, sea lettuce in particular, then the energy of light on these algae will increase the alkalinity of the pool so much so that some forms of seaweed will not be present in the pool i.e. red seaweeds, because the alkalinity is too high. Green seaweed is usually thin and looks ferny and delicate. By far the brown seaweeds are the ones we see and know best. In Angus, we call them 'tangles', thick stemmed seaweed with flattened ends and divided up into small straps. In the deeper pools by the outer rocks, they may seem to float with the movement of the tide. However the tangle very cleverly attaches itself to rocks with its foot called a holdfast. After heavy seas we may see this seaweed on the beach still attached to its rock.

Sugar kelp (Laminaria saccharina to give it its posh name) has a long narrow frilly blade like a fern and if you taste it, you will find it rather sweet. Fishermen in days gone by used it to tell if the weather was to be good or bad. They dried it and if the blade stayed dry, it meant good weather. If it went soggy and sticky like glue, it meant heavy rain, possibly even stormy weather.

The Bladder wrack is the one we all know for it covers the rocks and is the one we walk over. The little bladders are gas filled and keep the plant buoyant so when the tide comes in, it floats up to the light.

The spiral wrack doesn't have bladders, it has 'U' shaped seed pods at its tip and is mainly found up the shore a little way, sometimes attached to wooden posts etc. used for tying up boats. The channelled wrack at a quick glance is similar to the spiral wrack but, on closer examination, is much different. It has a curved hollow in its stem and traps the water between itself and the stones or rocks thereby it can survive without the sea for some days, if higher up the shore.

The red seaweeds live mainly in deep water but there are a few species to look out for in shallow water although usually quite small.

The two red seaweeds which are very similar are Carragheen and Gigartina stellata. The former, a reddish plant with small flat fronds, is pretty tough although edible. The latter, much darker almost purple, is usually in clumps and joined at the base. However Gigartina stellata has a secret. A jelly can be prepared from it called 'Agar-Agar' and is used for bacteria culture, medicine, silks, paper and cooking for soups and jellies. I believe it was discovered during the war, out of necessity. Agar-Agar came originally from Japan therefore another source had to be found. Luckily it was found in quantity around the British shores and proved to be of good quality.

There are tiny creatures in the pools such as Springtails, a tiny insect with little legs. You will notice it floating on the surface of the pool or on the seaweed. Another is the sea slater, much like the garden variety, found under pebbles. The worms you will see will probably be the 'tube' or

Lugworms and the most familiar is the ragworm. You will no doubt have seen the keel worms as dried little white tube bodies on pebbles and shells.

Occasionally, 'Barnacles' a crustaceous animal will be found in the pool, swept from a ship's hull and many will be attached to whelks.

There is however something else in the pool which, although classed as animal, really does resemble plants. The anemone is one such animal and can be red or brown. I believe there is a green one but personally, I have not seen it in these waters. The tentacles come out when the tide comes in and the animals sting their prey of tiny fish. They live on rocks and sometimes on wooden supports. Another anemone is one that lives half buried in mud or sand. Touch it gently with a stick and it will totally disappear. I have only seen the brown tube anemone but I believe colours are also red or white.

It is exciting when suddenly, you spot a slight movement out of the corner of your eye. It is a rock goby, a fish of about four and a half inches. They are not in every pool but you may be lucky. It is a brown colour and it has the ability to stick itself to a rock when the waves are more tempestuous.

It has been some time since I have seen the common Jellyfish washed up on the beach here but it used to be a common occurrence. However you may notice one from time to time in a rock pool, its transparent body throbbing as it moves. At the edge of the body are the stinging tentacles but these seldom hurt humans however small fish and baby crabs are stupefied by the sting and are then quickly eaten. England, particularly on the south coast, has larger Jellyfish and they do give quite a powerful sting so it is wise to leave well alone.

Crabs are such a joy to watch and the three you might meet are the Shore, Hermit and the Velvet crabs. The shore crab is just over 3 inches and can be green or red. Sometimes you will pick up a discarded shell on the beach; most likely it will have been eaten by fish or sea birds. I have watched seagulls pick up a crab and drop it from some height on to a hard surface and swoop down to eat the delicacy of soft flesh.

The velvet crab is much the same size but has soft velvet hairs on its shell along with strong blue and red markings. When disturbed, it stares at you with bright red eyes and its front pincers open up, telling you to keep away or else!

The crab with the perfect accommodation has to be the Hermit crab. As he grows, he borrows an empty mollusc shell, usually a whelk and reverses himself inside, by doing so he is protecting his soft body within the shell. He moves about with his front claws taking his home with him until he decides to move on to a larger hotel.

A rock pool would not be complete without molluscs from the tiny ones to strings of mussels, whelks and razor shells. These are extremely ancient sea animals at least 400 million years old. Apart from the mussels, the ones you regularly see have been vacated by their occupants, the bivalves with its two shells hinged together and the univalves with one shell.

Looking into the pool, the bivalves would possibly be cockle shells albeit unhinged; certainly mussels, sand gaper shaped like a cockle but smaller, mostly white and smooth; perhaps a razor shell and maybe if you are lucky, a scallop shell, perhaps the queen which is the smaller variety. Mussels are of course very common and are normally in clusters, the thin threads can be seen to be attaching each mussel so as to stay together. When opened, the lining of each shell is in mother of pearl. With all these bivalves, invariably we only get the one half but it is enough to give us some understanding of the adventurous journey undertaken by an animal that could be held in the palm of your hand. The univalves are the 'one' shell variety and are the shell that most summer visitors to the beach take home to remind them of their visit.

The whelk with its winding stair, its siphon for breathing and detecting food is a favourite and, as a child, I really believed I could hear the sea when I put the shell to my ear – perhaps I still do.

The limpet with its tepee shaped shell is again wonderful architecture; this is design at the highest level and yet natural simplicity at its core. The limpet attaches itself to rocks so much so that even the strongest wave cannot prise it loose. It wanders up to three feet from its spot on the rock to feed, scraping algae off the rocks. But the amazing part is that it goes home to the exact same spot from whence it began its journey. Various colours of winkles/periwinkles will catch your eye. They have no siphon to capture their food because they eat seaweed.

The other shells I would hope you would see are the lovely grey or painted top shell with its mother of pearl; the tower shell like a small corkscrew, and the beautiful little cowrie. Unfortunately these are seen less and less in our rock pools and beaches today.

As I gaze into the rock pool, I do wonder how all these beautiful fragile creatures can possibly survive in this wild element of wind and sea with its continuing tides but they have learnt to adapt in their world. Perhaps this is nature's true legacy.

limpets

Razor shell, whelk, cowrie, periwinkle, top shell

25

LIFE AT THE FIT O' THE TOON

I was born just before the Second World War ended, a time when memories lingered on in the minds of many. The aftermath of a country picking itself up and getting on with life must have been immensely difficult. For some it would never be the same but I was fortunate, all my family survived. Having said that, the scars of mind, body and separation played out for more than a decade. Reminiscences are more than just a 'bit of history'; they are the experiences of life. The tide had turned but living in the late 40s and 50s after the war was, for my parent's generation, hard but people had optimism, the fight now was for a better future. I feel that I was privileged to be part of that indomitable spirit and because of them; I was free to belong to my generation.

I class myself as having been advantaged living at the Fit o' the Toon, among a tight band of women whose life and core was living at the edge of the sea. They had been independent for a very long time prior to both world wars. Theirs was a different kind of independence; they were not fighting for equal pay, education or university degrees to make their way in the world. That was a bridge too far. These women knew what to do, knew that the brother, father or husband depended on them, needed them for their livelihood. Fisher boy married fisher lass because he knew, she knew, how their life had to be when making a living from the sea. The men went out into dangerous waters but it was the women that held the home, the family and workload together.

There is no doubt that the Second World War gave many women a chance to escape servitude employment and grossly underpaid workplaces only to be back where they started at the end of the conflict. However, in many women, the spark had been lit and they went on to fight for better jobs and the equality of women.

Unfortunately as in many things social background plays a large part and that included the sea-faring community. Ship owner to dock worker, captain to deck hand, skipper to fisherman. The one thing that tied all together was the sea, for it was master to all. Many a time in the winter storms, the boats would be tied up big and small for a day, a week, even a fortnight. That meant no pay. Worse, it could bring about death; the sea does not differentiate between social classes.

Ladyloan was home to me in the 40s and 50s. Kyd Street, Millgate Loan, West Mary Street and Seagate, the latter about as close as you could get to the beach. Many times wild seas would wash over the high walls at the rear of the houses but I recall only very occasionally did the water touch the buildings.

I had just started Old Ladyloan School but I remember so well Granny's small one room fisherman's cottage at Seagate. It was only a few years after the war, a shortage of housing and the living conditions were different then but, as a 'wee bit thing', I didn't notice the hardships. Granny's toilet was outside and her water collected from a 'wallee', outside tap; the pipes froze often. Whereas children took this in their stride, it was hard on the adults but when you have never had the luxury of a bathroom as now, you don't know to miss it. I loved Gran's big tin bath, placed in front of the large fire range. The water heated in huge pots on top of the fire. You were as warm as toast! Gran's place was never cold; the range was on as we say now "24/7". She had a tiny built in scullery and divided by a wall was a large built-in feather bed. There was only one way in but it was so high, Gran kept steps under the bed and used them to reach the bed; except my way of course. From the other side of the room, night-dress billowing, I made a run for it – SPLAT – right into the middle of the bed. What fun! Once I nearly went too far and just missed knocking myself out against the back wall.

Those nights I spent with Gran were wonderful. Even at eight or nine years of age and no longer bomb diving the feather bed – more's the pity – Gran would sit in her large Windsor chair in front of the range and tell me stories of when she was little and growing up in Kyd Street. I was enthralled. I would have loved to have seen the harbour full of ships with sails and rigging, schooners and luggers as Gran called them. Those were the days before fishermen had been enticed from Auchmithie to Arbroath. The days of the 'trade' ships and the arrival of the railways. The ships exported grain, salt, fish and the famous Carmyllie paving stones although it became known as the 'Arbroath Pavement'. These sailing ships brought in iron, flax and timber from Scandinavia and Russia. I recall the railway lines from the Catherine Street side of the Keptie Station to the 'Shore' although long unused by the 50s, they were still in evidence.

Gran's stories were real enough. My great uncle and her father, my great grandfather had both been Master Mariners and great grandfather also a navigator. Together and individually, they had sailed all over the world including the Mediterranean, East and West Indies and South America, in later times being iced up in the Baltic for many months at a time.

I had learnt the pride they took in their ships and their love affair with the sea. Always impatient to return, something Gran could not understand as a child, only later did she realise that the sea breeds these kinds of men and although coming home was joyous, the passion was played out with sea and the elements.

However the decline had begun, the railways expanded and steam ships were now the modern means of transport and too large for Arbroath harbour, berthing in Dundee, Liverpool and London. By the 1890s, fishermen had moved from Auchmithie and the Fife coast to Arbroath and the harbour was filled with Fyfie fishing boats for the 'sma-line fishing'.

By 1913, Arbroath had a thriving fleet and industry. Boats now were mixed, some motor driven but the smaller harbours still favoured sail. The First World War changed many things and the relatively singular world of fishing became a distant memory to many. The women carried on as best as they could but life was difficult. Their men were away in ships, some would never return. Others became a statistic from the mud fields of the Somme and Ypres. How can you and I begin to understand their fragmented and broken lives having never experienced their suffering and sorrow especially on such a scale? However Arbroath's Fit o' the Toon did recover and the fishing community became influential whereas other older fishing communities faded as a memory.

Unfortunately, it was not to last for some markets had already gone with the war and the herring fishing was in decline. Some of those young men who had returned from the war no longer wished or could because of injury to follow their fathers to the sea. The years of conflict had changed their perception of life. They had seen much and the nightmares told their own story. They no longer needed nor wanted to fight the sea on a daily basis but to be free to walk up the mountain just to walk down the other side.

Some women also had had enough and were glad if their men-folk went into other industries or indeed decided life on the other side of the world was for them.

It was at this time, late 1920s and early 1930s that the traditional 'Fit o' the Toon' community was slowly changing. Living by the harbour was not so important nor marriage between fishing families. The old traditions were slowly losing hold. Schooling was better and opportunities were there to be grasped. However the sea-faring community still had their identity which held well into the 1950s and early 1960s.

By the early 1950s, the identifiable dress of the fisherwomen was almost a thing of the past. There were times however when 'the gear' was brought out from the blanket box. The plaid shawl, the heavy navy pleated skirt called a blue coat, the strippit apron with concealed pocket, the flowery blouse and the knitted cardigan. No coat for fisher women seldom wore them. On these occasions, the women were going on their annual bus trip, dressed as they or their mothers would have been in days gone by. The other annual occasion was the pageant when processions of floats (open sided lorries) were dressed up to represent various industries or historical events. The fishing and the re-enactment of past events at the Abbey were always popular. The fishing boats would wear their bunting and flags. Hundreds of people would wait at the quay to go on to the fishing boats for a trip out to the Ness. At the end of the day, the drama was played out within the Abbey to commemorate the signing of the Declaration of Arbroath 1320, seats being provided in tiers as the Edinburgh Tattoo does today. The clothes would be carefully washed and pressed and carefully put away for another year.

Although the 'garb' was no longer worn, in the 1950s some women continued to 'bait the line' for the sma' line fishing. The boats were still mixed, line and net fishing but this had its own problems and ones we are familiar with today - 'over fishing'. Prices had increased for fuel and bait and there was now a lack of women baiters. The young women were no longer willing to do such arduous boring work. Many of them had seen their mothers and grandmothers do this routine work which took many hours. During and after the Second World War, many things changed even more so than the First World War.

My mother's brother was in the Merchant Navy prior to the war; was married to a fisher-lass whose family had come from Auchmithie. She had 'baited the line' for her father for many years. At the outbreak of war, my uncle changed from the Merchant Navy to the Royal Navy and, at the end of the war when demobbed, became a fisherman on a sma' line boat. In contrast, his sister my Mum worked at 'Shanks' painting the famous lawn mowers. This became a shell and bomb (munition) factory during the war. I have always had the deepest respect for her and all those women for the job they did, heavy demanding and sometimes dangerous work and she was only 5 foot 2 inches.

Living at the Fit o' the Toon was no barrier now for the population of the town had almost doubled. At various times soldiers, sailors, air-crew, nurses and many of their attachments helped swell the town by thousands. It was at this time, 1943, that Mum met a soldier who would become my Dad. He had been, prior to the war, a stone-mason and would eventually spend many years working on the Arbroath Abbey.

The fishing way of life for me personally had ended before it had begun but living in Seagate was a constant reminder of where I had come from and that I had a strong tie to this way of life. Grandfather had died in 1947 having taken a dizzy turn close the harbour edge where he fell on to a boat at low tide. Apart from having multiple fractures, it was found he had advanced TB. He died as he would have wished, at the harbour at the Fit o' the Toon.

To bait a line took experience, time and patience. The photograph in this book shows a long flat basket called a 'scull'. This was used to set a fishing line with eventually 1300/1400 barbed hooks. My own experience ended up with a hook through my finger which my aunt had to push through to be free of the barb ending – say no more. From then on, I watched my aunt and my cousin, a girl slightly older then me aged nine or ten, sitting in a cold stone lobby firstly shelling thousands of mussels which were kept in buckets of cold water. The mussels had been collected earlier from the carrier. Unfortunately, Arbroath did not have its own mussel bed so they were brought from Montrose and Broughty Ferry. Later they came from Morecombe in England. Apart from these being superb mussels, there was now a shortage of collectors here in Angus due to better paid work elsewhere.

My aunt was an expert, so quick your eyes could hardly keep up with her. The shelling and attaching the mussels, two or three to each hook which were about 2 feet apart on the line, would take anything from five to six hours. The scull's flat end would be propped up on a chair or stool, the baiter sat on a small stool and the line either in a fish basket or another empty scull. As they baited the hooks, they would 'set the line' so that it ran freely off the scull and not get tangled up leaving the boat. The scull, now baited, had to be kept cool particularly in warmer weather thus the reason for fishing by this method mainly Autumn to Winter and net fishing April to October approximately. An old bit of line was tied across the scull through the handles for transport which, in my day, was by cartie, a wooden fish box suspended on two wheels usually from an old pram and two long pieces of wood either side of the fish box for the handles. The fisherman's meals were wrapped up carefully and put inside the box and then the scull was placed across the fish box. The women of the family pushed it down to the boat. I have it on good authority that, in older days, the scull was carried by the women on their backs to the harbour.

There were set times for the boats to leave and return. In the Winter this was approximately two hours before low water and in the Summer, the boats left about dawn, weather dependant.

Sma' line caught fish were always favoured for it did not damage the fish. 'Sma' of course did not mean the length of the line rather its thickness. Fish caught this way were haddock used for smokies and finnans, flukes and whiting. When the catches of fish landed at the harbour, especially around 4 to 4.30pm, there was always great activity. Selling and bidding took place on the quay usually in the lee side of the harbour below the harbour wall. Once unloaded, the boat would sail across to the other side of the harbour to allow off-loading by the next boat. On weekdays, I would run from Old Ladyloan school to the harbour via the 'Ropey' or Inchcape Park if the tide was in and hope the old dock gates were closed because it took longer if they were open having to run around the dock.

Each member of the crew had supplied a scull and the proceeds of the catch were shared. Each man had one share, the skipper one and the boat had one share. A catch given to each man to eat; mostly haddock but crabs and lobster were not uncommon. Needless to say, I was brought up on a fish diet and was extremely fortunate.

My aunt's house was called a biggin'; a large flat upstairs and two small flats downstairs one on either side of the stone entry (passageway). We shared the washhouse, the outside toilet and each had a coal-house.

The one item that was very personal to my aunt was the smokie barrel. Many fisher women had their independence because of this unique piece of equipment. Many times I saw her bidding for a box or two of haddock down at the harbour. The fish would then be readied for turning into smokies. The smokie barrel, square in this case, formed a pit in the ground four foot deep approximately and four foot by four foot. The buried pit protruded about six inches above the ground and was lined with six foot oak planks all the way round. The pit would be lit and fed by small oak logs and it would smoke furiously. On top of the pit would be placed several five foot by two inch triangle sticks. Salted haddock tied in pairs were placed over the sticks with damp hessian sacks placed over the fish. These would take about forty to forty five minutes to cook. When cooled, the fish would be wrapped and placed in the creel (a large basket). We would often assist my aunt by turning the sticks and keeping the hessian damp. When finished, we would smell like a 'smokie', certainly very woody. For our assistance, my aunt would let us help ourselves to the broken haddock, accidentally fallen, now smoked and sometimes a little burnt. It was delicious! What would today's Health and Safety laws think of that; just think of what we would have missed!

The old name for a creel was a rip and worn on the back with a canvas strap across the chest. They often carried a smaller creel over their arm for, at times, they would have the odd crab or some finnans. These would also be smoked but the difference was smokies (the smoked haddock) remained closed with the main bone remaining but finnans were opened and boned.

The creels would be ready to go and my aunt would set off after delivery of the scull to the harbour. In some cases, the eldest daughter would prepare breakfast and see the kids off to school. Our good fortune was that we all had breakfast at Gran's including my parents.

The fisher women went by train, bus and some even walked to their destination to sell their fish. My aunt went to Forfar but then had to walk to some rural customers. The weather made little difference; rain or snow she would still somehow get through to her loyal customers. In the summer her daughter, my cousin, from about eleven years old went with her to ease the weight for the creel was heavy. In days gone by, this would have been to gain experience preparing the way for doing her own round but the fishing community knew that this way of life was ending and that it would not be necessary to teach the young women a life style that had sustained them for over 200 hundred years. Motor vehicles were now delivering to Dundee, Perth, Forfar and the rural areas. Trains and buses were subject to change and some areas lost their station altogether. Government legislation would finally end the fisher women's sojourn.

The late 50s saw a bill introduced that stated when dealing with food; a washing source had to be provided for hand washing. This was something of course the women could not provide and, in the end, the vans won because they could in essence carry water and a basin. I wonder just how many of these vans carried out the letter of the law.

However, not be deterred, the fisher women carried on smoking their fish. Now they were running a business from home, selling to the public direct or selling to shops. They were determined to hold on to their independence and, to many, a second income was a necessity.

Given any free time, most fisher women were to be seen knitting the famous ganzy used by the fishermen to keep them warm at sea. Made with wool treated to be waterproof and usually dyed navy blue, they had 3 or 4 buttons down the side of the neck. The patterns in the jumpers told a story; the battle with rough seas, welcoming harbours, of life in olden times and of lost loves but always about the sea. My mum knitted several for me and I had them for many years. I remember when I got it wet on more than one occasion when walking in the glens of Angus, it had a strong lingering smell of rain and the open air. My lighter clothes underneath this jumper were as dry as a bone. A few years later when walking in Greece, I wandered into a shop in Athens by the harbour and the Greek lady immediately threw up her hands in delight. I had a ganzy jumper on and, in broken English, she was able to tell the story knitted into my jumper. It is truly universal, the sea connects many people in different ways.

The fisherman's day was 10 to 12 hours at sea hauling in the nets many times. The catch was different from that of sma' line fishing. It would be plaice, dabs, skate and sometimes even catfish. It was pleasing if the men had time to check the nets and mend them if need be on the journey home. Or if sma' line fishing, it was preferable to have time to check for lost hooks and frayed lines. The scull and line would then be ready for the baiter. All saved time. With the gear stored away, it meant that after the unloading of the fish, it was only the hold and deck to wash down and the men could get home. This was not always possible especially if the sea was wild.

There was little leisure time at the Fit o' the Toon in the 50s. Life was learnt the hard way. There were few line boats equipped with navigational gadgets. Life on board was every man knowing his job and experience was what kept them in wages and alive.

At times, no matter how much experience you had, the sea would claim its own as it did on the 27th October 1953 when the lifeboat 'Robert Lindsay' went down with six brave crew. Having gone out on a tempest sea with the purpose of rescue it was to no avail for they found neither boat nor person. They did what was asked of them. On their return, they themselves ran into difficulties. The rocket had sounded; the Fit o' the Toon alerted. Doors flung open. It was approximately 5am. Men ran to the harbour, some women followed, others sat and waited for news. My family was there that dreadful night. The sea tossed the lifeboat this way and that. Lines fired in the darkness were caught in the wind and came back empty with the exception of one and one man was saved. The boat was being battered on the bar but could not cross to quieter waters. In the end, it was flung and held fast on to the end of the bar. The morning after on the way to school as always I went by the Signal Tower and Ropey and there was the 'Robert Lindsay' lying on the rocks. My friend was not with me that morning for her Dad had died that night. It has been 60 years but I will remember it always. The shell of the lifeboat was taken to Mackays' boat building yard. There was a need also to collect the small broken pieces of wood from the 'Robert Lindsay' that had been thrown up on the beach. These were also taken to the boat yard and placed by the boat slip wall where they lay reverently for many years undisturbed.

Although those involved will carry that night forever hauntingly hearing the various cries for help, many are no longer here themselves and memory does become distant. Those that were unborn then will know of it but it was a tragedy not of their time. The lifeboat itself has undergone change; it sails proudly again in new waters in the South of England.

I spent many happy hours at the water when young. I hardly ever wore shoes in the summer and running across the stones or rocks when the tide was out was not a problem. Limpets, buckies (winkles) were never felt. Summer was full of halcyon days spent at the beach, the harbour or walking with my dog around the cliffs to Seaton or Auchmithie. Fishing for crabs was a great pastime. A piece of string, smallish stone tied on the end, a few shelled limpets tied on about four inches apart and you were set. When the tide had gone out exposing 200 yards or so of rocks, you went out and found a good rock pool that was about 5 or 6 feet deep. In went the fishing line and within minutes out would come the crabs, large and small. They were lifted off and placed in another pool. We never harmed them. It was all about the number of crabs you could catch before the tide turned. My friends and I had no fear of the water. We respected the sea and were in awe of its power.

Like many at the Fit o' the Toon, I learnt to swim at an early age. 'Danger Point' at the bottom of the High Street was also a playground to us. The bridge over the Brothock Water was used as country kids used a tree and a rope to swing into the water or to get over to the other side of a river. We had a rope tied under the bridge which was used in the same way. Coming from the beach, it was easier to swing over the water than to climb up the rungs of a rusty ladder cut into a twenty foot high 19th century wall. Steps had been cut into the harbour bar at the other side so it was easy to scramble up those to the cobbled road and on to the harbour. In those days of course you could walk along the top of the bar. This is not permitted these days. Only at certain places have railings been provided so that visitors may have a view of the sea. This small space is usually occupied by men and women rod fishing particularly at mackerel time. Walking along the bar on a clam evening was magic. The scene and the light on the water were probably captured countless times by many artists. At any one time I would count eight, nine or ten of them, many no doubt went on to greatness, some obscurity; artists endeavouring to capture a moment in time which I now realise I and others from the Fit o' the Toon witnessed every day.

In the earlier days, it was the habit of several churches and missions of the town to take it in turn to give a sunset service at the harbour on a Sunday evening in the summer. Visitors and locals seemed to enjoy this and were usually in fine voice. If the tide was low, the cadences would resound off the harbour wall as an echo. You could hear the voices across the other side of the harbour. As the visitors drifted away in the gloaming, Jimmy the 'leerie man' would arrive to light the gas street lamps at the shore. Sometimes I felt these lamps gave out a haunted and eerie circle of blue light especially if the sea fog had rolled in with the tide. Usually I gave way to an ancient terror and ran home to the safety and welcome of the cottage. The gas for homes and street lights was locally manufactured from Ponderlaw Gas Works. I remember taking my cartie on a Saturday morning to the gas works and collecting cinders for our fire. In the early sixties, the last of these lights were gone; they had served their time and we now had electricity. One of my abiding memories was the weekly arrival of Smith & Hood's coal cart because it was pulled by a lovely docile Clydesdale horse. The coalman, Tam Robb I thing was his name, kept him in immaculate condition and looked after his welfare. He would only allow him to pull a certain load and always on the flat. There were no hills at the Fit o' the Toon to speak of anyway. In icy weather, the horse was not used. Instead the firm would use their motor vehicle. When this lovely horse retired, he was not replaced but was much missed by us children for his gentle ways and eager acceptance of a slice of bread or an apple.

The harbour and beach are full of birds; it is their home. They have always shared their place with us but in today's world, we grudge them what morsel they might be given. Notices have been erected telling us not to feed the gulls. The people of the Fit o' the Toon have been feeding gulls for decades. The fisher women when gutting the fish placed all the heads and inners into a bucket and carried it to the beach to feed the birds. It was a two way relationship with no waste. Perhaps the notices should be for humans.

Looking out of the window this December day, it encourages me to feel reflective. I look towards the hills now not the sea but my heart will always belong to the shore.

The seasons come and go in the Angus glens and I know the landscape will recapture its joyful youth and yet diminish in intensity all in the same year. The Fit o' the Toon is different in its seasons but equally pronounced. In days now long gone, a walk along the beach particularly after a storm would have yielded much sea-drenched wood which, collected and dried, made wonderful kindling and seaweed for a salad or the garden. Buckies (winkles) gathered and when cooked were a wonderful snack. I used to sell them to visitors to the harbour for sixpence (in old money) a jam-jar. Beautiful shells lay waiting for you to find with which to listen to the sea or perhaps make a necklace or bangle. Music created by the sea was dependent on the season. From the soft lapping against the sand in Spring, the gentle whisper in summer, the sweeping waves with dancing spray in the autumn to the thunderous crash in winter; the sound of pebbles being lifted and thrown against rocks in a restless sea. If sympathetic to the sea and its ways, you will be aware of its rhythm and movement, the crescendo and pianissimo, a musical score created by nature.

My family's love affair with the sea started long, long before my birth. It has weaved its magic for many generations. It can be remote, wild, fragile but always forgiving.

'Ropey'   The beach in front of the Signal Tower so called because of the long narrow sheds that once stood there for rope making.

'Shore'   In many households at the Fit o' the Toon, this meant the harbour, not necessarily the beach.

'Biggin'   A two storey flatted house

Evening at the Harbour, Arbroath.

THE WATCH TOWER, ARBROATH.

Scull as used at the Fit o' the Toon

BLOWING AWAY THE COBWEBS

For those who enjoy the temptation of intriguing beaches, hidden caves, perilous sea stacks and beguiling views out to sea whether in high summer or the bitter cold of winter, one of the best cliff top walks in Angus lies at the edge of the coastal fishing town of Arbroath. At the eastern end of the Victoria Park, a snaking path at the Ness, or Nes as it was originally spelt, leads up to the top of ancient Devonian red sandstone cliffs. In front of these cliffs lie treacherous flat rocks or skerries exposed at low tide; a favourite stance of shags and cormorants as they stand with wings outstretched like silk sheets drying in the wind. These rocks may look a delightful place to roam but beware – the tide comes in very quickly and there is no escape for the unsuspecting wanderer.

Back on the cliff top track and around the corner from the Ness looking over the cliff edge to the shore-line below, at low tide it is easy to see the remnants of early 19th century cart tracks made by workmen collecting stone from the Ness Quarry when Arbroath's third harbour was being built. The story goes that while gathering the stone, workmen accidentally opened up a crack in the rocks revealing the entrance to a cavern hidden by fallen rocks for many years. Scrambling inside, they found two chambers; one around 300 feet in length and the other some 100 feet in length. During their exploration it was said they found incredible stalactites hanging down from the roof spaces totally untouched. Regrettably the stalactites have long since disappeared no doubt at the hand of man leaving only the name The Stalactite Cave to remind us of its once breathtaking past.

Up above, the well-trodden path with its banks of thrift, sea campion and tufted vetch continues around the top of the cliffs. On one side, fields once full of grazing sheep are now used for the cultivation of soft fruit. Curlews, crows, peewits and pigeons forage there while around the sheer cliff faces, black backed gulls, common gulls, herring gulls and black-headed gulls swoop, calling incessantly while acrobatically diving with ease and dexterity. It is so sad to know that these wonderful birds, once the friend of fishermen and fisher folk are now on the endangered list. Shags and cormorants fly low across the grey water and on the shoreline, sandpipers, dunlins and turnstones noisily scurry among the rocks and sand in pursuit of food while oyster catchers flock to the shore line to bathe in eager anticipation of their forthcoming meal on the incoming tide. Wild flowers happily inhabit the rocky crevices impervious to the elements, their only fear that man may pick its delicate flowers to extinction if too readily accessible. If the walker is very fortunate, a pod of dolphin may be sighted leaping in and out of the water further out to sea, enjoying a local feast of fish as they swim up the coast.

To the right now lies The Needle's E'e, a superb natural arch lying parallel with the coastline. With its incessant pounding, the sea gradually wore out a cave in the sandstone until the continual erosion caused the rear of the cave to collapse leaving this amazing arch. Fragile it may be but even on the coldest winter day, fishermen can be seen casting for mackerel. It is worth remembering however that storm force winds at high tide cause waves to crash through the Needle's E'e with a ferocity man cannot compete with.

Lying to the left of this sandstone sculpture is a little beach called "Mermaid's Kirk" or as it is known locally Pebbly Den. Enclosed and covered with shingle; the sea reaches this beach through a tunnel in the cliff. As the tide ebbs and flows, the noise generated by the waves on the pebbles echoes through the tunnel creating a thunderous roar particularly spectacular at high tide.

On a tranquil day, it is easy to be lulled into a sense of quiet serenity with blue skies, gentle waves and male sky larks high above singing their little hearts out to their loved ones below but when the harsh wind furiously blows and heavy seas constantly lash the sandstone cliffs, tearing at the cliff's very soul, it isn't hard to understand why the next cove is called the Mariner's Grave. In days gone by, the cove was the scene of a shipwreck in which some of the ill-fated crew were lost. The story goes that the few lucky survivors were hoisted to safety by rescuers using ropes lowered over the cliff edge. Until fairly recently, the grooves made by these same ropes on the edge of the cliffs were re-cut from time to time by men from Arbroath.

Following the path, on a very high tide with gale force winds, a spectacular display may be seen from the Blow Hole as sea spray blows ferociously through the hole. However, great care must always be taken if venturing off the path at any place on the walk as the weather has rapidly worn away the conglomerate, revealing soft crumbling sandy soil making the cliff edge and face very dangerous. It is therefore safer to watch this wondrous display from a distance. Rabbit holes and gorse bushes also need to be taken into consideration!

The path now turns inland taking the walker around a long sea inlet called Dickmont's or Dickman's Den. Said to be named after a smuggler called Dickman who perished there after his boat was wrecked on the formidable rocks, the long inlet with its distinct echo and mass of rock in the centre has always been linked with smuggling, a part of everyday life in days gone by. Prearranged signals with the smugglers were common; sometimes it was a small fire lit on an isolated beach or an enormous washing hung on a line. Smugglers risked life and limb to land their illicit cargo of French wines and strong spirits at night with many stories told of how they avoided the dreaded excise men. One story was of wives sitting on upturned fish boxes containing the smuggled goods while rocking their babes to sleep right in front of the excise men!

In springtime, the verges and sides of Dickmont's Den are clothed in wild primroses which, for a while, were rarely seen as the plants were plundered by walkers. Now with such rapid erosion, the sides are too steep to venture down thankfully allowing the primroses to safely grow in abundance as nature intended giving a creamy glow to the sometimes dark ravine.

From Dickman's Den, the track passes a superb sea stack known as the Deil's Heid. The power of the waves driven by the majestic sea has eroded much of the cliff around the stack leaving it standing in splendid isolation and a haven for sea birds. The space between the cliff and the "Heid" is known locally as Duncan's Door; a landmark of fishermen and mariners as it looks, from certain angles, like an open door.

Passing gorse and broom, sea thrift and red campion, harebells and sedums, the path continues its way north-east while underneath, more caves abound. One such is known as The Doo Cave or Dove Cave as it is inhabited by pigeons. All the while, the views out over the sea to the Bell Rock Lighthouse, itself a magnificent feat of engineering, are stunning.   One or two small fishing boats from Arbroath may still be seen, surrounded by gulls hoping for a friendly helping hand-out of fish, the only time these birds seem to be allowed near man these days without being chased and hounded from their natural habitats for the wrong reasons.

On reaching the next headland, a lovely beach of pebbles and sand comes into view, a steep grassy path leading down to the shore.   From here, The Mason's Cave so called because the St Thomas Lodge of Freemasons were reputed to meet annually on St John's Day for the admission of members, may be reached at low tide.   What else went on there was never revealed!

Up above this cave on the headland lie the vestiges of an ancient fort called "The Maiden Castle".   The name appears in the Chartulary of the Abbey of Arbroath and may go back as far as Iron Age times but sadly like much around this area, little archaeology of note has ever been done and may be lost for all time.   From here, a spectacular example of cliff erosion has left a rocky headland called The Three Sisters or The Sphinx and the Camel's Back.   From certain angles, it is an apt name.

It is at this point that the walker is faced with various choices.   Turning left a path takes you back to Arbroath via East Seaton Farm with its plethora of fruit bearing polytunnels; retracing the cliff-top path; walking further around the bay and up Seaton Den to the tarmac road and back to Arbroath or carrying on to Auchmithie.   Whatever the decision, it is worth noting that somewhere in this area lay Cove Haven. It is thought that back in the 1700s or perhaps even earlier, there had been a small fishing village with houses or fishing huts both down on the beach and up on the cliff-top.   According to John Thomson's Atlas of Scotland 1832 however, only two buildings on the cliff-top were still surviving at that time. The sea with its ever-changing moods and colours would no doubt have claimed those on the shore. By the 1850s according to Marine Charts, it appears these two buildings were in ruins and nowadays, there is nothing to be seen, no mark or sign to indicate that a small fishing community had ever inhabited the area; only two words on a map – Cove Haven. Perhaps it lay between the Deil's Heid and The Three Sisters or perhaps more likely in Carlingheugh Bay where there were fresh water wells and a tributary of the Seaton Burn, thus ensuring a fresh water supply for the fisher folk of Cove Haven.

The now rapid erosion of these 400 million year old cliffs is evident for all to see and care is always required particularly if walking with a dog or small child but with its breath-taking views and scenery, this cliff top walk is worthy of taking during all the seasons and hopefully with Angus Council and Scottish Natural Heritage's help, it will continue to be enjoyed for generations to come.

Remnants of early 19th century cart tracks

Bank of thrift and wild flowers

LUNAN BAY

I have always loved Lunan Bay and it is easy to get carried away and see in ones mind's eye the Vikings running up the beach pilfering as they went and carrying away feloniously goods from the local people.

Lunan Bay is a place kept secret from most tourists for decades. The lovely sandy beach stretches for three miles although the bay itself is five miles wide. Over time, the sea and wind have altered the contours of this place. The soft silvery dunes can be eerily quiet, at other times the minute grains of disintegrated rock are tossed in the air, disturbing and changing the shape of the shore-line. Waves attack the beach relentlessly and are far stronger than the returning tide leaving the sand dunes in a fragile state. The winter gales easily throw these temporary sand hills into a state of flux.

The name 'Lunan' suggests that it may have come from the word 'Loun', a Scots word meaning quiet, calm or sheltered and it is likely many ships would have taken refuge in the bay in stormy weather. Then again, the old Gaelic name for the place was 'Lounan' meaning boggy marshland and it certainly was that; however most of that has gone now.

I walk down the 'C' road to Lunan. It is early summer and a beautiful morning. I catch a glimpse of the ruined Red Castle on the hill. If only walls could talk, what secrets, what history they could tell us. I pass a few scattered houses which had been fishermen's crofts at one time, now brought into the 21st century with double glazing, extensions and solar panels. The narrow stone bridge has to be negotiated by walkers with care these days as cars take up practically the whole of its narrow width. However it is worth the risk to look down into the waters of the River Lunan on its way to meet and greet the sea. Tiny splashes indicate that there are fish in the river but the salmon are long gone now.

My view takes in two fairly large buildings other than the castle, Lunan House and Home Farm. There is no doubting that it is a rural place, no Post Office, no pub, no shops, only a small church occupying the site of an earlier pre-reformation building. Lunan is a timeless place with a rough beauty to match.

Over the years, Lunan has mainly been a haunt of locals from Montrose, Arbroath and surrounding areas with a sprinkling of holiday makers. Early 20th Century saw Lunan House become a private hotel but even then it was far from a fashionable resort. Its sandy beach lies mostly empty. I must admit selfishly for me that is its attraction.

As I walk by the Lunan River, I reflect how peaceful it is in this modern day and anyone not knowing its history would think only that it was a lovely place, a quiet sleepy hollow without realising it has been touched throughout the centuries by so many people's lives in so many ways. Kings and Cardinal have shared the journey along with merchants, fishermen, farm workers, crafts people, labourers and smugglers. Little is left physically on the landscape but the echoes of the past are all around.

Human bones have been found in the Lunan district dating back to 1700BC, late Stone Age. The hunting grounds were possibly on higher ground at Rossie Moor, two or three miles North West of the bay on ground away from the area of estuaries and rivers. With meat and fish available, trees and reeds for houses, it is no wonder hunter-gathers stayed. Settlements spread and villages were born.

Forming a natural harbour, the tidal basin, the town of Montrose was destined to be: it grew from a small village in the 9th/10th century into a busy town known for its mills and salt. By the 11th and 12th century, it was entertaining Royalty. A castle which may have been of wood stood at the southern end of the High Street. William the Lion 1143-1214 possibly used it as a Royal residence when performing Royal duties. However, when at leisure, it is thought that his love of Angus drew him to Lunan Bay Castle. He in fact granted this building to his chamberlain Walter de Berkeley sometime before the late 12th century. Castle lands were of antiquity and relate to Anglo-Saxon nobility so there may have been a building on the site long before William's time. I have to wonder perhaps, again, if it had been a timber building originally and used as a retreat for hunting but also it was so well placed, as a look-out for Norse invaders. The named land surrounding the castle leads us to believe that royalty was indeed present. We have Courthill, known to have held the courts of justice and Hawkhill, the home of the King's falconer.

Walter de Berkeley's daughter married into the Anglo-Norman house of Balliols. So, if my history serves me well, another king was to have the soil or sand of Lunan beneath his feet albeit briefly.

The castle bears its name from rubeum castrum which comes from a deed written in 1286 thereby some stone-work must have been present at this time. Unfortunately these days the building is in a dangerous condition and is in a gradual weakening state. It is still exciting to view and to feel that we are following in the footsteps of our forebears and already we have become a part of the social history of this place. The history of the Red Castle is a little vague between mid-13th century and 16th century. We do know that Sir Andrew Campbell resigned his interest in the barony in 1367 and it was granted by David II to Sir Robert Stewart of Invermeath. It remained with this family until the close of 16th century when Lord Invermeath ceased to reside at the castle.

Archaeology tells us that the castle was added to and strengthened between the 13th and 16th centuries. The ruin gives little impression now of the actual size of the building and its importance. The rampart was almost 24 feet high and 6 feet thick and nearly 100 feet long on the west side; the north side was 23 feet long. A tower had been added, possibly 15th century, whose walls were 6 feet thick and measured 44 feet by 33 feet and standing at 50 feet.

It is unreasonable to think that Lord Invermeath, owner of Lunan Estate and the Abbot of Arbroath, David Beaton, would not have known and dined together. Both were of the period; both well-travelled and lived a stone's throw from each other. The Cardinal as he was to become in 1538 lived in Ethie Castle with Marion Ogilvy who was reputed to be mother of their eight children. Marion Ogilvy (Lady of Melgund) was the daughter of James, first Lord Ogilvy of Airlie.

We must not judge David Beaton too harshly for many Catholic servants of the church lived in circumstances no different from a married couple. If a church career was what was intended then official marriage was out of the question. David Beaton became Archbishop of St Andrews in 1539 but he retained Ethie.

Unfortunately the 1530s and 40s were troubled times and Henry VIII and the reformation altered things forever. David Beaton did not survive the reformation for he was assassinated at St Andrews in 1546, his naked body hung on the castle wall and left to rot. However Marion and the children remained in the Angus area and had been left well provided.

In the spring of 1579, the Red Castle was attacked by a son of the Gray family of Dunninald Castle, the father being Sheriff of Forfar. The son, Andrew Gray, was known as Black Jack from his reputation as a middle class pirate. It is said he lived in a fortress on a cliff top at the north end of Lunan Bay by Boddin Point. He and his followers attacked the castle and set fire to it. Lord Invermeath was away at the time but Lady Invermeath, his wife and mother were present, escaping only by hiding in the tower. Black Jack ran off with the contents of the castle and set fire to the outer range. He returned to the castle in February 1581, plundering and setting fire to the building. Fortunately the owners were all away this time. He was arrested and his fortress home was partially destroyed.

As to Lunan Castle, the Stewarts of Invermeath did some repairs and it was habitable. They remained in possession until the end of the 16th century when it was passed to the Ruthvens of Gardyne and then to the Earl of Northesk and finally to the Estate of Panmure. It was last occupied still in fairly good condition to the end of the 17th century but it had had its time and, in 1748, roofless and robbed of its life blood, its stones, we reach the final chapter. The sea wind has reduced its shell even further and I wonder how long the remaining pitted curtain wall will stand.

With this summer's day the sea looks inviting. I keep to the dune path as the tide climbs further up the beach.

There is a botanical interest in the dunes at Lunan Bay. The lovely Campanula rotundifolia (Harebell) leans over the path, the blue bell flowers touching the gravel, Buttercups and Lady's bedstraw tolerating the windblown sand. Lunan has a temperate climate and this coast is well known for sunshine but the light winds can blow from the sea on warm spring days and bring in the haar.

In the distance is the fishing hamlet of Ethiehaven nestling in to the bottom of a sandstone cliff. An important fishing village in the 18th century, its way of life began to deteriorate by 1850. With no proper harbour and new design of boats, larger and with more capacity; it struggled alongside places like Montrose and Auchmithie as a safe refuge.

There is no proper road to Ethiehaven and no signpost guides your way. As a walker from Lunan Bay, you may reach this place by the sands and on up the cliff path for the headland walk to the Red Head, Auchmithie and on to Arbroath. Once, your view from the hilltop would have taken in the privileged sight of puffins, guillemots and gannets fishing but no longer. If you are fortunate, you may see a family or two of puffins or guillemots but the gannets no longer come to feed. They have all moved on and unfortunately, bird numbers generally are in decline.

I sit and watch a wagtail as it runs across the grass of a small oasis in the sea of sand by the river. This small bird walks and runs unlike its friends the sparrow, chaffinch and blackbird who hop over the grass. It is searching for food, invisible to me but obviously plentiful within the grass. It darts into the air alighting a few inches further on. What grace and elegance and what joy to watch this little ballerina on this summer's day.

I turn to view the river and catch a glimpse of the black and white dipper. It settles on a stone jutting out of the water and then, in an instant, has disappeared below the water. There it is again; its flight has now taken it around the bend of the river and from my view. I must retrace my steps now and begin my journey home. I no longer live close to this special place but I promise with a wave to sea, beach and river that I will return when I can, perhaps in a different season when the days are shorter but the light is generous and sparkles with frost.

With winter approaching, I manage a few days at Lunan Bay. Not a soul is stirring, the ground under my feet crunches with heavy frost. I inhale the tang of the sea and the snell east wind hits me. Scanning the bay, I can understand on such a day a smuggler might take a chance to come ashore with a few bottles of wine. However early 18th century merchants and landowners of Angus smuggled on a much larger scale tobacco, tea, fine wine, coffee, currants, earthenware, soap, guns to name but a few. Their ships would leave local ports on their way to France, Italy, the Mediterranean and beyond. The ships were full of legal salmon to export but not so on the return journey. Many of the old shops and houses and of course pubs/inns in Montrose, Arbroath and Forfar had cellars and wine vaults to hide these goods from the tax man. They even imported cork so that the casks of wine could be bottled and corked. Some of these merchants and landowners, upstanding members of the Kirk, went one step further. They had easy made wealth on their minds so they turned to slavery. Their ships carried salmon to the Mediterranean and when off-loaded, the ships were temporarily internally altered to take black slaves. After crossing the Atlantic, the slaves were sold and the ships internal layout restored, scrubbed down and filled with tobacco. In its remoteness, time has dimmed this cruel act of humanity but its shadow will always be present.

Around this time, so the story goes, a young lad by the name of William Imrie journeyed down from Aberdeenshire. Feeling tired and weary, he rested by the

River Lunan at Lunan Bay. Falling asleep, he dreamt that one day he would return to Lunan and own this place. He journeyed on to London and after some years of travel to places like India, his business thrived and he became very successful and very wealthy. However he never forgot his dream and returned to Scotland around 1759 and bought the Lunan Estate. The old House of Lunan was pulled down and the building standing today was built around 1825 and enlarged in 1850 or so. It was also about this time that he added to his name and became known as 'Blair-Imrie'. This was sometimes done for reasons of inheritance. The latter part of the story at least is true for the family lived at Lunan House until possibly the late 1930s early 1940s when it became a private hotel. I believe the grounds and gardens were laid out by the Blair-Imrie family. Although simplistic in design, the gardens were reputed to be beautiful, the lawns and trees sweeping down to the river. Unfortunately I have been unable to track down a copy of Robert Haddleston's book published circa 1790 'A Tour from Arbroath to Montrose' which included Lunan Bay. It would have made interesting reading. William Blair-Imrie invited Robert Haddleston to come to Lunan Parish in 1789 as schoolmaster so he would have got to know the people and area well.

Everything is approaching its winter sleep and the daylight hours are brief now. The robin sings her sweet song as she stands on the branches of the Himalayan Balsam. This invasive plant dominates the river front and without control can eventually choke the river. I must admit it is beautiful at this time covered in droplets of frozen rain, icicles forming like mini stalactites. A few rose hips still remain also covered in hoar-frost, a favourite of the Anglo-Saxons as a winter fruit. I am following mounds of frozen earth as a mole has been active here by the river. I crouch down low as the sand dunes give a barrier to the very cold wind. I am watchful of the sharp Marram grass, a survivor of dry conditions and wild winds. My footsteps will have been heard and all will be quiet underground. The casual visitor will not often see this velvet creature although he does not hibernate; he has a time and place for his entrance to the world we live in. I walk beyond his digging. If he hears no ground quivers from above, he will go on about his business.

Lunan is such a joy and I am so glad the idea back in the 1880s did not materialise. A proposal for large villas some 300 feet from the sea was suggested with fishing, golf course and curling thrown into the mix. It never happened – what an escape. The 19th century was probably the most recent of workers, weavers, carpenters, blacksmiths even a shoemaker; all are gone now. Nature has been left to do its own thing. The salmon fishermen are still here, a small number now, the nets can still be seen drying in the wind. Over the years, the means of travel has also altered. From shank's pony to horse and cart, stage-coach, changing no doubt at the Old Chance Inn, a posting house at Inverkeilor. The train service arrived and taking the journey from Arbroath to Montrose, you could alight at Lunan Bay for it had its own station and station masters house in the days of 1883. It is difficult to see any remains of where this actually was but if you look on an early 20th century map; it was quite close to the present line. Lunan Station was closed to passengers in 1932 and goods 1965. The car is now master of the road but parking is a premium, another reason for Lunan to remain a secret gem of the North East.

Lunan also had its part to play during both 1st and 2nd World Wars. The Red Castle was used as a look-out station.

Concrete pill boxes were built for use by the Home Guard. Meanwhile growing the nation's crops was a priority. Chivers & Sons arrived in Montrose after the 1st World War in 1925 to manufacture their jams and jellies, also canning fruit and vegetables. They rented many farms and land in the Lunan area including Home Farm and Courthill Farm for the duration of the 2nd World War.

Lunan Bay was again to take centre stage just before the 1st World War. The first British air station was set up at Upper Dysart Farm, close to Lunan Bay. It became operational in February 1913; its main job was to closely monitor German Zeppelins who were on spying missions. On the day of 27 May 1913, pilot Desmond Arthurs' bi-plane disintegrated mid-air and he fell over 1000 feet to his death at Lunan Bay. Unfortunately there was no safety apparatus worn in those days. I mention this incident because Desmond Arthurs' name is synonymous with the ghostly apparitions that constantly appear not at Lunan Bay or Upper Dysart but at Broomfield, slightly north of Montrose. The air-field was transferred to there in January 1914 as the Upper Dysart was found to be unsuitable some 9 months after Desmond Arthurs' death. A visit to the Montrose Air Station Heritage Centre should not be missed. I leave you to ponder on that one!!!

The Lunan Hotel lingered on for some time. I myself stayed there in the 1960s. However it is now the 'Lunan House Care Home' and I can think of no better geographical location for such a place.

Delicate snowflakes are beginning to fall but the salty sea-air will melt these beautiful crystals soon. My eyes water with the wind coupled with a tear of having to say goodbye to such a lovely place.

Red Castle in silhouette

Red Castle

Lunan water with boats

THE AGATE COAST

The Angus coast is wild and rugged; the old red sandstone rocks are many millions of years old now shaped into sculptures by the wind and sea. These rocks are made up of sandstone and conglomerates, occasionally shale. The lava within the sandstone is where the agates occur and is called amygdaloido. The lava contained gas bubbles and filled with calcite, quartz, agate and chlorite. The rough agate stone you may find is millions of years in the making, laid down and created long before man walked this earth. Most agates have quartz at their heart and a banding of chalcedony layer. This is thin bands of a variety of quartz and colours vary mostly white, grey, brown or even light blue. There are many different types of agate but those found here on the Angus coast are mostly pink and brown with the exception of the beautiful Blue Hole agates but more about that later. There are occasions when you will search the beach and find small broken rock and it will show you markings as described but invariably, the amateur hunter of agates will be wise to know what kind of pebble to look for as the rewards can be rich indeed.

There is however a code of practice in searching for agates for your safety as well as the environment. It is wise not to go hammering at cliffs as you may well end up with tons of rock on top of you. If walking the beach, it is easy in your enjoyment to forget the time and, in certain areas, you could get cut off by the incoming tide. Try to collect fallen material from the beach rather than hacking at the larger rocks.

I am at Boddin, a few miles south of Montrose. This has been a salmon station for many years, well before the revolutionary farming technology began. I refer to 'limestone' found at Boddin. In the late 16th century early 17th century, it was discovered that placing lime on the fields increased grain quality and quantity. Thus a limekiln was built at Boddin in 1696/97 but proved far too small and quickly the demand was outstripping the supply. The limekiln we see today was built by Robert Scott around 1750. The sea and shore are places of constant change and the limekiln, no longer used, stands to lose its fight against the elements. Now cracking badly, notices have been erected warning to keep away. The slipway too has its problems. Nature as the unformed artist either leaves havoc behind or a thing of wild beauty. The cottages used by the limestone workers are now in ruins, but there is something unsullied about them. Fiercely independent and in the shadow of the cliff, they face the invasive sea.

I wander on to the beach and begin my search for agates. After an hour or so, I have found one or two hopeful agate rocks; you never really know what you are going to find inside the pebble.

I return to the headland and take the path to 'Elephant Rock', so called because the sea-worn sculpture looks like an elephant although in days gone by, the details were perhaps more clearly defined. The true name of the giant rock is St Skae and, as I pass this place, it is a reminder of nature's constant battle, the primeval elements against man's daring optimism for sitting on the very edge of this rock is the remains of a burial ground. Once compact within its walls, now graves and stones are lost to the sea. If you feel so inclined and are feeling fit, there is a path down to the beach at low tide. The humble pebble draws you down; seek for they are there for the passionate researcher.

My next port of call is 'Usan' or to use one of its old names 'Ullishaven', the spelling different each time the name was put to paper. Usan is a natural harbour and has been a fishing community probably from time immemorial. It was first recorded in 1548 but a cadger road apparently existed between Usan and Forfar to supply fish to the Royal Court when in Forfar. As Forfar ceased to be a favourite with William the Lion's sons late 13th century, a fishing village must have been there before then. However it was possible in those early days the village also housed farm workers. Although the remains of houses are still visible, just, they were built around 1822 by the laird at that time. This was a single row of 28 houses built of local stone and lime, thus replacing the clay and thatch cottages of a much earlier time. A tower was built and used by the Coastguard from 1835 along with a few of the new houses. The remainder of the houses were for salt workers, custom officers and fishermen. These salt pans were set up at Usan in the late 18th century and the salt sold mainly to Montrose. English rock salt began finding its way into Scotland and selling more cheaply than Usan could harvest it so unfortunately the operation closed around 1830.

Gradually the population of Usan dropped with losses in the First World War and people moving to Ferryden. Some of the houses were let out as weekend and holiday cottages a few remaining to fishermen. Although salmon fishing went on in the 18th and 19th centuries, perhaps even earlier, it was never the main occupation. However salmon and crab fishing has now taken over Usan. Wooden huts on the beach, rusty winders, old tractors, even old cars were in evidence the day I was there. The houses have been left to decay and are all derelict now.

I am not dwelling on that today as my destination is the beach and the crème de la crème for agate hunting. Usan has long been associated with agates particularly 'The Blue Hole'. Discovered in the 19th century by Robert Miln and Professor Matthew Heddle, the exact locality has now been lost although some say not entirely and that it is known to a few professional collectors!

To see the best of these blue hole agates, we must go to the National Museum of Scotland as both collectors, Robert Miln and Professor Heddle, donated their collections to this museum. These agates when viewed are breathtakingly beautiful although not all blue and white as might be thought as yellow and red are amongst those found. It is to these stunning blue agates that we are drawn. These agates, when cut, can give the impression of a seascape and the skin of the rock a frame.

Some years ago a friendly local told me he thought the cave or hole had just collapsed and that there was always a chance that loose agates would find their way out. Cherish such statements because that is what fortifies the amateur collector. Agates have been collected and polished from this part of the coast since at least the 18th century and a man called Eelbeck, a stone polisher, was particularly well known. So keep looking for the blue agates but if they prove elusive, the others will more than compensate.

I head now for the Mains of Usan. The cliffs have gone and the rough flat grass meets the rocks and stony beach. The limestone is in evidence here along with the lava rocks. Wild grasses grow with the salt bearing lichen in different colours. It is difficult to keep my eyes fixed to the pebbles for the birds are calling and taking flight as I disturb their sleep or feeding patterns. The eiders male and female are in abundance, a few shelducks are about and that wonderful sounding bird, the curlew with its haunting cries.

I am almost at the 'Mains' with its island of rocks called 'Sillo Craig' meaning a crag or rocky place. Deserted buildings echo the past and I wonder what stories they could tell. Simple and elemental things I am sure when the pageant of nature was the most important thing in peoples' lives for they lived and died by it. It is this abandonment that enriches the perception of the place.

The sign directs me to 'Sandy Braes' a mere 500m and further to the lighthouse at 1200m. One or two cars are parked by the farm, gone fishing probably or beach-combing. This farmer is very tolerant of cars and people so it must be remembered to tread gently through the given path beside the crops and give the cows their place without interruption. Gates are closed for a reason, to keep in or to keep out. We have the freedom to access and go through; the charge is simply to close the gate behind you.

The sea is on the turn and the gulls are watchful for incoming snacks. I stop and listen to the music of the sea. At this phase of the tide, the sound is soft and distant and yet I know, with the approaching waves, the sound will gather in momentum into a crescendo as the sea climbs the beach and attempts to overwhelm the land. The concert of the sea is remarkable for different notes are played each time for the wind, stones and sand are never in the same place. I have picked up several small agates, already broken and shaped by an angry sea. The brown, pink quartz is already easy to spot.

Scurdyness lighthouse is now in my sights. A tall building built on shore rocks at the entrance to Montrose harbour; a building when built in 1870 gave hope and certain relief to mariners. It joins the Bellrock Lighthouse to endeavour to save lives.

Scurdie was converted to work automatically in 1987. Progress can be tinged sometimes with regret as I am sure the lighthouse keepers will have been when they set the light for the very last time. Visitors can gain entry to the lighthouse but be prepared to climb some 170 or so steps for your view. You can, if desired, walk the last half mile on the lighthouse road to Ferryden. The road gives you a slight advantage to the beautiful view of harbour, bridges and beyond and you pass Second World War memories of gun stations and pill boxes which are still in evidence.

I continue to trawl the beach although the afternoon sun is sinking and a breeze is picking up from the incoming tide. The water reflects the crimson light of the dying sun and I can see into the fairly shallow channel. The larger boats await entry to this safe haven. My rucksack is getting heavier now and I rejoice in what pleasure it will give when arriving home to examine the stones. Some will disappoint but others may turn out to be exquisite.

My friend has parked the car at Ferryden so I may now reflect and impart my day with a welcoming flask of coffee.

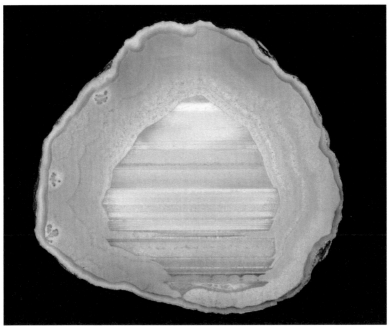

Blue Hole Agate © National Museums Scotland

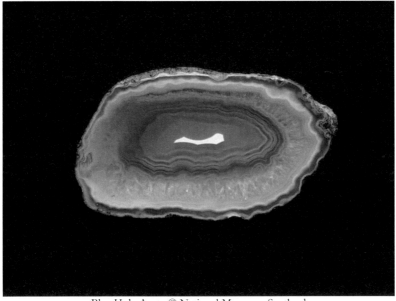

Blue Hole Agate © National Museums Scotland

Usan, Near Montrose.

MONTROSE, SCURDYNESS LIGHTHOUSE
49930

PART TWO

QUIET ABSENCE

THE FLYING HORSE LINE

In the glorious age of sail when dockyards, ports and harbours all over Britain were bursting with ships from all around the world, Arbroath, like most coastal towns, was not only a very busy fishing port; a hive of industry and commerce, particularly for those who lived at the Fit O' the Toon but was gaining a distinguished and world famous reputation for its sail-cloth and canvas. There were several important textile families in the town but one in particular made sure their name would be synonymous with quality and that was David Corsar and Sons. The family had lived in Arbroath for many decades and, at the turn of the 19th century, started business by way of hand loom weaving. With their spinning and weaving business expanding, in 1823 they bought the old Nursery Mill. In 1848, they constructed the Spring Garden Works, the first power-loom factory in the town. The Applegate Factory soon followed and with their flax spinning business expanding along with their workforce, by the second half of the 19th century; the company employed a workforce of around 600 people.

The surname of Corsar is apparently of French origin; reputed to be the occupational name of 'the cosser', a dealer in horses. From their family crest, the Corsars adapted the horse motif into their House Flag; a blue square with a flying horse in the centre and the firm's initials D.C. & S. in each corner, all in white. On each bale of canvas and on every sail they made; the word 'Reliance' was stencilled with the flying horse motif underneath.

The mid-19th century saw Arbroath's harbour becoming so busy; ships had to take it in turn to offload their cargo, mainly raw flax from the Baltic. Around the docks and boat building yards were rope works, granaries, coal sheds and, of course, taverns where tales from the sea-farers were legend; tales not only of foreign lands but of life on the high seas. Just off the docks, the peaceful little chapel would fill with young and old, asking for safe passage and a safe return to their loved ones as they were about to embark on another voyage. Outside amid the constant hubbub, horse drawn carts pushed their way through the hustle and bustle of the quayside; herring gulls swooped and soared, at home among the forest of masts of these magnificent boats as they gracefully searched for tasty morsels from the fishermen off-loading their catch nearby. The fishermen all wore blue 'ganzies', a thick hand knitted jumper with buttons on one side worn on top of shirts with no collars. These jumpers of oiled wool were so waterproof; they could be taken off, shaken and put back on leaving the wearer dry and warm. The same garments were all hand-knitted by mothers, grandmothers and wives and each one told its own tales for these men, whether dumpy, skinny, tall or short were all born to the sea. They and their families before and after them all lived at the Fit o' the Toon. It was their kingdom and the romance of the sea was in their bones.

There is no doubting the sheer elegance and grace of the windjammers with their 3 to 5 masts and square sails and it is little wonder they became known as the grandest of all the merchant sailing ships but for the men on board these magnificent vessels, it was seldom an easy life. From flat calms to raging storms, the fearsome elements paid no heed to status whereby apprentice boys, cooks, cabin boys, mates, carpenters, ordinary seamen, navigators and captains alike could be tossed into the seething water and pulled down without mercy to its icy depths fathoms below. Wearing 'all in one' boiler suits made of rubber without sleeves and big sea boots, there was little chance of survival as the suits quickly filled with water dragging the wearer down among the hidden creatures of the deep. Travelling the world, these sailors never knew how long a voyage may be or what might happen for it wasn't only the weather they had to contend with but illness and death. They never knew if they would return although perhaps some did not want to, hoping instead to find a better life overseas in distant lands. Disease was rife with scurvy the plaque of sailors until it was apparently discovered by a physician of the British Fleet in the West Indies that lime-juice could prevent scurvy. The British Board of Trade thereafter ruled that at midday, all sailors were given a pannikin of lime juice; not exactly the sailors drink of choice. The name "lime-juicers" or "limeys" thus came into being for all British seamen.

The call for sail-cloth and canvas from Arbroath grew with tales abounding of its superiority, one in particular being of a British man o' war coming through the Bay of Biscay in a hurricane with every one of her sails ripped to shreds bar one, a staysail that remained intact. That sail was the only one woven and stitched in Arbroath. In the tenements and houses around the town, the clattering of hand-looms could be heard through all the hours with whole families involved including children.

Such was the demand for the town's sail-cloth and canvas, it was perhaps a natural progression for Corsars to enter the world of shipping themselves.

In 1858, a 174 ton North American schooner called 'Haidee' had come into Arbroath Harbour to off-load its cargo perhaps of flax or hemp, oak and fir timber or flour and tea. This vessel became the Corsar's first purchase and it plied their trade successfully for several years. Corsars now had the ideal platform on which to continue their thriving business of selling canvas. They already sold some of their canvas from their Liverpool office where their agents were the firm of Dixon and Wynne who later became W T Dixon and Sons, merchants and shipbrokers.

By 1861, Corsars had sold the Haidee in South Shields. Its replacement was a brand new vessel of 237 tons called the Princess Alice. Built for Corsars, it was the first ship they had owned from new. In the Arbroath Guide and County of Forfar Advertiser dated July 13th 1861, the following announcement was made.

"On Wednesday July 11 1861, the Princess Alice, a three masted schooner was launched from the yard of Messrs J & J Hall, Arbroath. This new vessel is the property of Messrs David Corsar and Sons and was named by Mrs William Hannay Corsar."

It isn't hard to image the euphoria at the launching among the workforce of David Corsar and Sons. The Princess Alice sailed all around the world from Riga, the capital of Latvia; Cronstadt, the port of St Petersburg, Russia; to Denmark and Sweden, South Africa and beyond, returning to London, Dundee, Tayport and Arbroath.

Arbroath's mariners were as well known around the world as the 'Reliance' canvas and none more so than Captain William Sim, born in Arbroath in 1836. Captain Sim became a legend in his own lifetime for his excellence of seamanship and the highest possible standards of efficiency in his profession. His first command was in Yokohama and, from a family source, it is stated that Captain Sim would not sail unless his brother George, a Master Seaman in his own right, went on board as his navigator. Together their reputation for navigation, cleanliness and order of their ships preceded them. They sailed regularly to Rio de Janeiro and the South American ports. At some point, they took over the running of the Princess Alice bringing her into Arbroath on the Far Eastern tea run from China. When she had berthed, the two brothers were treated like celebrities with the vast crowds gathered to cheer them home, parting to allow them to walk ashore. It is also said of the Princess Alice that there was no prettier boat in the harbour in her day.

The Princess Alice was wrecked at Port Natal on 31 July 1872 during a ferocious gale while carrying a cargo of timber from Sweden.

She was certainly not the only vessel to be owned by David Corsar and Sons but the Princess Alice was the only one built in Arbroath. The ships built for the flax trade had to be much bigger and have the ability to cut through ice. As Arbroath's harbour was not big enough to hold these larger vessels, the shipping section of Corsars business transferred to Liverpool. All of Corsars ships after the Princess Alice were therefore built elsewhere; in Glasgow, Liverpool, Sunderland and Dumbarton, as well as overseas but all were registered in Liverpool with W T Dixon & Sons initially running the business for Corsars.

From 1869 onwards, like all trading companies, ships were bought and sold according to their needs. From the Melpomene, built by Reid of Glasgow in 1869 to the W H Corsar, a wooden ship of 1410 tons built by Brown & Crowe in Maitland, Nova Scotia and purchased by Corsars in 1879. The Malta and the George Roper, a four-mast barque wrecked on her maiden voyage on the Lonsdale Reef were both bought in 1883. In keeping with their Scottish roots however, some of David Corsar & Sons vessels were very Scottish in name. The Glencaird, built by Russell of Port Glasgow in 1889; Cairniehill again built by Russell of Port Glasgow in 1889; Fairport and Musselcrag both built at Port Glasgow in 1896 and one of their most famous, the Monkbarns, built in 1895 by McMillan of Dumbarton. The last three names were apparently inspired by Sir Walter Scott's "The Antiquary". There were other ships, The Tasmanian, Edith, Almora, Dartford and Chiltonford but the two that really made the shipping world sit up and take notice were the Pegasus and Reliance built in 1884 by W H Potter of Liverpool for they were the first sailing ships to have their officers' quarters amidships. These two magnificent four masted ships were carriers rather than record breakers taking coal, nitrate and timber across to Australia and to the Pacific Coast. The Reliance however caught fire while carrying a nitrate cargo in 1907 and was burnt out but her charred hull was bought, rebuilt and renamed Ricart de Soler after the man who invested in her. She continued in service until 1924 by then under the Spanish flag and renamed Iberia when she was finally broken up.

It is probable that with the launch of the Pegasus came the introduction of the Corsars famous figurehead. Painted white, the beautifully carved figurehead of a flying horse brought together not only the motto stencilled on every bolt of their canvas but also that of their family crest. Pegasus was famed as the winged horse therefore it was only fitting for this ship to have such a figurehead. The Corsar merchant shipping line was thereafter known throughout the world as "The Flying Horse Line".

The Pegasus remained with Corsars until 1909 when she was sold to Neilson and Co of Larvick, Norway. In 1912, whilst carrying a cargo of lumber, she was stranded during a heavy gale and three days later, having been successfully towed into Reval, she was condemned and broken up.

By all accounts, of the four carriers the Almora, Fairport, Monkbarns and Musselcrag launched under Corsar's Flying Horse Line in the 1890s, it was the Monkbarns that was the finest sailing ship.

One of the last sailing ships under the Red Ensign, the appropriate flag worn by British merchant ships; she had many adventures during her life-time. Her sailing times were fast. On one of her trips from San Francisco to Falmouth in 1904, she took a mere 110 days, beating many other 'faster' ships. She also had her share of tragedies. In 1906 while on her way out to San Francisco, she was caught in an ice field to the south of Cape Horn during the depths of winter. She was frozen in for 63 days in bitter Antarctic weather during which time her skipper, Captain Robinson, died. In 1926, she was sailing from Valparaiso in Chile but had to put into Rio de Janeiro in order to land her Captain who had become seriously ill. He died in Rio but the ship carried on arriving in Gravesend in 1926, 99 days later under the command of her first officer.

For all the men who sailed in waters far and near during the 19th century, they must have felt safer knowing their ships' sails were made by the sail and canvas makers of Arbroath. When David Corsar and Sons finally closed its doors, the legacy this Arbroath company left behind was enormous. Without the quality of workmanship, the skill and craftsmanship of the workforce in Arbroath, the seas would have been an even more dangerous place in which to sail.

The Corsars were not only familiar employers in Arbroath; they were well thought of and respected as individuals whether it be in the Arbroath Literary Club, the

Rifle Volunteers or playing cricket for Arbroath Cricket Club. Charles W Corsar was in fact its first Captain. James Corsar, a partner in the firm of David Corsar and Sons and a big, rather stout man, was known for his bright cheery manner. James and Peter, his two sons who were also in the family business, were well known in Arbroath as cricketers on the West Common with James Corsar junior being an outstanding member of the United Cricket Club in Arbroath.

David Corsar, who was Provost of Arbroath from 1867 to 1869, on his retiral bought the old High School from the School Board. He had it enlarged and entirely reconstructed to provide a lending library, reference library, large reading room and picture gallery which he then gave to the Magistrates and Town Council for the people of Arbroath. This building still stands today and is a much used and well-loved building in Arbroath.

By the late 20th century, with the closure and demolition of all the factories, weaving shops and mills, along with many of the traditional houses, Arbroath became a quiet town. With the Fit O' The Toon now subdued by the loss of most of its fishing industry, the harbour is mainly used as a marina for folks with their yachts. But stand still and look down into the harbour; look at its ancient walls. Watch those majestic gulls as they soar on the winds and turn your gaze out to sea. You might just catch a glimpse of the past, catch the smallest glimpse of a by-gone age when ships proudly sailed the world with the word "Reliance" stencilled on their sails and with the figurehead of a flying horse under their bowsprit.

Reliance Canvas
© Angus Cultural Services

Figurehead of flying horse on 'Monkbarns'
© Brown, Son & Ferguson Ltd, Glasgow

SPRINGFIELD HOUSE

It was mildly cold and a light southerly wind was blowing making the autumn leaves dance under the horses' hooves. The moon was full and the stars bright in the ocean called sky.

Doctor Thomas Stevenson M.D. was returning home to Springfield House Arbroath after a long tiring day. The drive gates were open and the house just yonder was welcoming.

The Stevensons were an old Arbroath family and he, Thomas, was a Fellow of the Royal College of Physicians in Edinburgh.

The date is in the 1790s and Springfield Estate and house, a red sandstone building, had had its birth probably mid 18th century. Ask a local of Arbroath where Springfield House was and they will probably look at you blankly but ask for Springfield Park and almost all will point you in the right direction. Unless you are over eighty years of age, Springfield will have been a park all of your life.

The house had been built probably by Thomas's father John as it was he that acquired the land. The location was superb, situated on a hilltop with beautiful views. The approach to the mansion house was by the small steep hill at the end of Hill Terrace; the entrance gate being prior to Academy Lane which in Thomas's time was actually part of his garden. Through the main gate with stables on the left, now closed toilets, on the right was the lodge, no longer there but the out-buildings still remain.

Moving past the walled garden, this central green island in front of you was the location of Springfield House with farm land beyond. It is unknown whether the buildings in Ponderlawfield at the south side of the street were tenanted by Springfield Estate or ground having been sold off at an earlier period. Certainly the Wesleyan Chapel was opened for worship by John Wesley on 6 May 1772 and the manse stood along side. There was a further gate house and estate houses further up Ponderlaw where a residential home, a Gospel hall and fire station are now situated. This entrance and avenue would also have been used by the employees who lived and worked on the estate. The dirt road would have been directly in front of the houses with their vegetable gardens over the other side of this road; an arrangement which was common in Scotland at this time. The small road in the early 1840s became known as Ponderlaw Lane; now of course the lane is no longer there having been built upon.

The estate continued with no further buildings in Ponderlaw at that time up to what is now Springfield Terrace, curving round into Cliffburn Road, passing today a residential home and into the park to the braes. The area in total would have covered approximately 29 acres, the house and the farmland beyond 25 acres, the house and garden roughly 4 acres.

It is known that Thomas Stevenson was a scholarly man and a kind and well liked Doctor. It was with sadness that, particularly with a young family, he died in the November of 1799 aged 38 years. The good Doctor had lost three of his children when they were in infancy but he left nine children all under fifteen years of age. Unfortunately there was further sorrow to come for his wife, Ann. A further eight children died before her, two in their teens, three in their thirties, two in their forties and one aged fifty three. Only one daughter 'Mary' survived her mother. Ann Adam Stevenson died on the 15th January 1847 aged eighty six, forty eight years after her husband.

The Georgian period is usually accepted as being 1714 to 1830 and Springfield House fits into this time-scale. It was a house of moderate size; a roomy two storey building with basement and attic with steps leading to the front entrance but it was unpretentious in architecture. The avenues around the house would have been shaded by fine trees and laid out in grass. Further trees may have sheltered the house and garden with a stone wall surrounding some or all of the estate. It is an age of high fashion pertaining to a style of architecture, dress, classical music and dinner parties. A house such as this suits the period admirably. The late wealthy Georgians appreciated landscape with many trees and the creation of shaped land, of ridges, hollows and troughs instead of long flat vistas. They were a society who appreciated functional things that actually worked but, at the same time, looked good and gave pleasure. For those who could afford it, luxury was an acceptance of the period in which they lived.

Looking back upon the Stevensons domestic arrangements, and no doubt they would have had the best, lighting for example would have been exceptionally poor to our standards today. In most homes in those days, artificial light would have been by lamp, the 'crusie' possibly hung by the chimney and filled with whale oil. However our middle class family would have used candles, probably wall mounted sconces, candelabra, ceramic candlesticks and lanterns but even then, it would have been under- lit.

The safety match was not patented until 1824 so the Stevensons staff would have lit the house fires by using a tinder-box, flints and sulphur. A slow and smelly process however a fire once lit in the kitchen was kept burning and used to light the various lamps and candles. Good candles were made of beeswax albeit costly but the smoke was less and the smell more pleasing. Remarkably because of the cost candles were still favoured over oil lamps at this time because of the dirt and their unreliability.

The late 18th century was a time when land values shot up in price and more land was being enclosed for agricultural improvement. The countryside began to change. There was less waste ground; fields having hedges and dry-stane dykes, more house building and roads. Arbroath was changing in earnest but in some cases not always for the better. Unfortunately, it was also a time of unrest as the inequality of the rich middle class and poor began to over step the bounds of impartiality.

It may have been in view of this and combined with most of her family's departure that Ann Stevenson decided to sell Springfield sometime between 1813 and 1820. The new owner was David Louson and he had taken over the reigns certainly by 1822 as shown on 'Woods' map of that time.

David Louson, son of a shoe-maker, was born in Arbroath 6 August 1781. He was to become a property owner, financial business man dealing in stocks and shares and was involved as a board member in the Arbroath and Forfar railway venture, a well respected banker who was to claim the title of Town Clerk of Arbroath for many years. It was probable that he was living at Woodville House prior to his marriage on the 6th June 1811 to Mary Colville.

Money he may have had but death is something we all share and, unfortunately, three of his children died in infancy. Death was not new to him as his mother had died when he was only 14 years old but, at this period late 18th century, he would have been expected to accept her death as a man not a boy. However a child Mary Ann was born on 3 October 1815 but their joy was short lived as Mary, his wife, died 8 November 1815 aged 23.

In the meantime, David apart from his professional career had been deputy town clerk for some years and had become the Town Clerk in the November of 1812. He paid the sum of £1000 for this position but this was an acceptable arrangement which Mr Hay of 'The History of Arbroath' fame informs us 'went to pay for the paving with cobbles that part of the High Street extending from Horner's Wynd (Commerce Street) to Lordburn.' This was an important position although unpaid but one that no doubt advanced his career in business and his standing in middle-class society. It was a union that was to last 46 years from 1812 until 1858.

David Louson married again in November 1822 to Anne Forbes Gleig, daughter of Reverend George and Mary Gleig. David's daughter Mary Ann age seven now had a step mother and, before long, a younger sister Mary Duncan born May 1824 joined by a further sister Jane born in July 1827. However Springfield House was to witness yet more pain. Anne, David's wife died November 1827 aged 33 years. Both wives dying so young, David himself now 46 years old and left to care for three daughters aged 12, 3 and 4 months; it was so very tragic but yet there was more to come. Jane, the youngest daughter died in November 1832 aged five.

This 'Regency' period as it was known was not really a style as such; it was the gentle decline of 'Georgian' albeit William IV was on the throne.

By 1833, David had extended the house and possibly with new ideas of the time had perhaps even installed a water closet, maybe more than one as was the fashion prevailing at this time. He had also no doubt taken advantage of the gas system that could now be pumped into the house. Arbroath businesses had had this option from 1826. The kitchen was not the heart of the home in the 18th and 19th centuries at least not to its owners. It was a hive of industry to those who worked there but at least it would have been warm with a cast iron cooking range and oven. Accompanied by a large table; sinks, dressers and shelves would have been fitted around the room and all surfaces would have been scrubbed almost white.

I am guessing there would have been an ice-house and it would have come into its own especially in the summer. Built of stone and sunk down in a shaded area, it would have kept wine, food and vegetables cool.

As much as we love bathing today in our candle lit bathrooms (out of choice) to stress-out; bathing in the 18th and early 19th century was not considered important nor had the word 'stressed' been invented. But trend was as equally important then as today. When it was proved that cleanliness helped to eradicate disease, those who could afford it wanted water by the bucketful. Slowly technology improved and hot water could be heated in the kitchen by a boiler, carried and brought up to fill a bath situated in the bedroom. Unfortunately the water had to be disposed of by the same means! Most Georgian bedrooms however, probably including Springfield House at this time would have had wooden wash stands and, for the ladies, a porcelain ewer and matching porcelain based. Hot water would have been brought up for their use; the chamber pot being concealed in some kind of cabinet.

The fireplaces were probably a simple affair, perhaps moulded plaster or plaster over pine and painted. Delft tiles were imported from Holland in the early 18th century but from 1750, Britain was making its own tiles. So the house may have had a mix of tiles and wallpaper as, by the 1790s, this was the new 'favourite'. People did not re-decorate as often as we do today and it was usually a 'royal' period that altered the style. In this case, it was Victoria coming to the throne in 1837. It was quite clear that all was changing and the next sixty odd years was quite definitely the 'Victorian' period.

Alterations were also afoot to close the back entrance to Springfield House (Ponderlaw Lane) and make this solely an entrance to the farm. A new main entrance was created close to the Methodist Manse which is used today to enter the park. A lodge was built and possibly a second stable for horses and carriage. The new avenue was lit perhaps by the new gas pipes laid from Ponderlaw to the house. It appears that further ground was released from the estate for what is now Springfield Terrace and this probably happened in the mid 1840s. Thereby the Free Church manse appeared followed by the Episcopal Church and manse of St Mary's commencing in 1852 and consecrated in August 1854 with the remaining ground in Springfield Terrace also being utilised around this period.

David's first child, Mary Ann, married Archibald Dudgeon, Merchant, in the February of 1839. It appears that they lived at Springfield House. Happy times for such sad memories past. His other daughter, Mary Duncan by his second wife Anne, married James Dickson, banker and magistrate in the December of 1844. They however went to live at David's property at Woodville.

Springfield House was in full flow and the latest addition was a large Victorian summer house added on to the south side of the house. I suspect this would have been a very enjoyable part of the house, comfortably laid out, possibly some new introduced plants that required some heat perhaps such as Camellia, Hibiscus, Begonias, Allamanda, Fuscias and not forgetting Ferns to name but a few and a lovely place for afternoon tea.

The garden had become the place for expression and it appears David took up this interest and entered the world of horticulture.

When you view Woods map of 1822 and again in the map of 1842, it clearly shows a circular border of flowers or box edging in front of the house perhaps acting as a circular driveway. However a map surveyed in 1859 by Captain Martin shows a sun dial in the centre of the 'roundabout'. It is difficult to know if this was a new addition by David Louson or it had been there in Stevenson's time but was seen as unimportant by previous cartographers.

However, David Louson did complete many other additions to the house and garden. He went on to extend the avenues and install pavilions where one might sit and take in the view whether it was towards the cliffs, the harbour, Ladyloan or indeed towards the Abbey. A further achievement comes to light shown on this same 1859 plan; that of a large walled garden with the possibility of even further plans for an extended garden around the house itself.

Scottish gardeners were held in high regard and many were head gardeners with the ability to lay out and create new gardens. By this date early to mid 19th century, there were many books describing how gardens should be made and with the knowledge of a good hands-on gardener and an owner who was also enthusiastic, the requirement of a landscape architect would not necessarily have been needed. The desire for a beautiful colourful garden was growing. The lawn, topiary and statue type of garden was on its way out even in Scotland although some large houses held on to these for long enough. But the progressive owner who was advocating change and wanted a more colourful landscape fell in love with the 'bedding' trend. A Victorian passion which has never been equalled, thousands of annuals were used on a large scale. The walled garden came into its own; parterre, kitchen borders, fruit and vegetable but undoubtedly dominated by massed planting of annuals.

Garden societies and magazines began in the early 19th century. 'The Memoirs of the Caledonian Horticultural Society' was published in 1827 and the 'Scottish Gardens' a little later in 1852.

The Springfield House gardens are not shown on the early map of 1822 apart from the driveway to the house. In 1842, the map shows an extended tree-lined driveway to Ponderlaw but, as yet, no walled garden. Thus is appears that the walled garden was created between 1842 and 1859 as is shown on the map of that date.

Unfortunately, it is difficult to know how the garden would have looked initially but it is probably a good guess that the basic hard landscaping plan would have followed the general trend of a walled garden of the period. What may have been different is the sitting out area almost in the centre of the garden as seen again on the 1859 plan. This may have been of wood, sandstone or even marble. There may have been a water feature in the garden so loved by Victorians but what ever the layout, it has all the hallmarks of this exciting time. The garden itself in its young days will undoubtedly have had roses and yet more roses, the passion of the time being the 'old double yellow' Ayrshire Rose and the hybrid Rosa spinosissima. Parterre will have played a part along with box edging, shrubs such Rhododendrons and Azaleas would have added great value to the other favoured green flowerless shrubs with seven or eight foot wide herbaceous borders setting the scene. Plants rooted in the past such as thyme, lavender, violets and favourites such as juniper, clove pinks, auriculas, anemones, sweet William and tulips will have been present.

Without an early record of the gardens particularly the walled garden, it can only be imagined but the feeling is that he wanted the best at the time for his home and family. Changes were coming in thick and fast in these heady days of Victoria's reign. The garden was no exception. Plant hunters, many from Scotland, were sending seeds and plants home every few months and society wanted them; the demand outstretching availability.

The Springfield walled garden would have changed. Some beloved flowers may have stayed and I personally believe the herbaceous borders remained with their perennials. It was however time to make way for the annuals; an explosion of colour giving this feeling of being intrinsically entwined with the paint-box of nature. Many of these plants are still favourites today; geraniums, violets, verbena, dahlias, calceolarias, lobelia, alyssum, sweet peas, salvia, hollyhocks, nasturtiums, pansy and many more. At this time in the late 1840s and 1850s, William Black, Head Gardener and his staff at Springfield would have had their work cut out for along with this mass planting, there would have been the house flowers, the Summer House and the fruit and vegetable gardens to deal with. The garden walks taken by the family and those who made it happen must have been uplifted by perfumes beyond price and, in the stillness of an evening, the wild honeysuckle, lavender and climbing roses would have been perfection.

A greenhouse may have been sited at the south west corner. This is however speculative although it was usual for a greenhouse to have been in a walled garden. It was often a 'lean-to' type placed on the south wall side of the north wall.   Grapes and particularly strawberries were a possibility for the greenhouse as they were in high demand and many pounds were eaten over the summer.   It is possible that another larger greenhouse was in use at the north end of the garden adjacent to Academy Lane. Remains of a boiler house, coal fired for such a structure, seems to have been in evidence at an early date.   Several entrances and exits are to be seen now blocked up in the walls surrounding the garden. The size of this walled garden was fairly large but this was an individual taste, in this case David Louson.   I am sure his daughter would have had some input however.   The walls at this time would have been made of plain stone, not ashlar dressed and set with lime mortar.   Although some of the walls are still remaining today, they have been knocked about a bit, added to, replaced and altered somewhat.   Brick was rare in Scotland before the mid 19th century.

There was a wall that was popular from the 1750s and that was the 'hot' wall.   It was a case of heating the wall by ovens and then a system of hollow walls was invented, where fires were lit, acting just like a chimney.   As time went on, furnaces took over by installing these below ground level and having flues built into the wall.   Unfortunately although it was of some benefit on a cold night, the problem would have been keeping an even temperature throughout.   This would have been nigh-on impossible, burning wood and coal.   The hot walls were used for fruit, particularly peaches. It is an idea that there may been such a wall at Springfield but its history alludes us.   However, it is fair to say that it was a strong possibility.

Outwith the walled garden, trees would have influenced the landscape; Scots pine, Spruce, Hollies and closer to the house may have been the 'Gean' Prunus avium. By the mid 1840s, conifers were the 'must have' and of course as previously mentioned, Scottish plant hunters were sending home seeds of Pinas ponderosa, Cupressus, Picea and Abies. One particular tree that was all the rage and everyone who was anyone wanted was the seed of the Monkey Puzzle (Araucaria araucana). Scotland lagged behind on this one due to the demand in England but it finally became available in 1844/45.

Now it is speculation that David Louson planted this particular tree but I would not be the least surprised if he had.

In nature, trees are the legacy when all else has gone and they provoke a strong yet delicate perfection, taking generations to develop and it is this profile we must consider when altering the landscape by cutting them down.

Mary Ann Dudgeon had lost her husband by 1851 and there were no children. By contrast, Mary her sister had seven, one of the boys being David Louson Dickson. I am sure David was a very proud grandfather.

Time was moving on for David and it comes to us all does it not that these twilight years are reflective of deeds done, opportunities missed, people we have met and touched our lives and loved ones that have gone before. David Louson had had plenty of all of these; high and lows, sadness and joy personally and professionally. I am sure he had met many notable people in his life-time but it is more difficult to pinpoint real celebrities that were to stand the test of time and also those who achieved deeds in his place of birth and the place he called home.

Perhaps Robert Stevenson, builder of the Bell Rock Lighthouse was one such person. David had been Deputy Town Clerk during the building work and it was something tremendous just to have been involved in this achievement even in the most humble way.

In a different way, Sir Walter Scott visiting the town in 1814 had a lasting effect and was memorable for the town as the 'Antiquary', published in 1816, was to many Red Lichties Arbroath immortalised.

The weather always seems to dominate our lives and it certainly did in the winter of 1822/23 when the worst snow storm in living memory hit Arbroath with people and animals frozen to death. Worse was to come. The first epidemic of Asiatic cholera had hit England in November 1831. Scotland followed and in 1832 it hit Arbroath. In those days it was a difficult disease to control as sanitary science of hygienic principles had not yet been applied particularly with drainage. Many people died particularly the old and the young. The suffering had a long-lasting effect in the town. David's own daughter died that year.

But there were sweet memories also; walks in a summer's evening through the garden with his eldest daughter Mary Ann, the lingering perfume of flowers and the lovely summer sound of the bees buzzing from flower to flower capturing the pollen before the petals closed at twilight. Such simple priceless things.

So it was on the morning of 11 December 1858 as the day awakened, the farmland shrouded in mist, wisps of colour tinged the sky, David Louson died aged 77 years. Now all was silent but spring time was near and the carefully tended wall garden would once again be liberated from its winter sleep and death would have a new beginning.

Mary is now alone but Springfield is her home and her father had left the house, grounds and farm to her. To his other daughter he left money to the value of Springfield House. David Louson had been considerably well off with a lot of property in Arbroath and England. Several rents and feus continued to be paid to his estate including the rent for Springfield farm which was tenanted out. He was however a very generous person and legacies were left to other family members, his house staff, gardener and various good causes. Springfield continued in much the same manner. Her father had left adequate funds for the house and garden to function and delight and Mary Ann was not, it seems an extravagant person.

In the July of 1866 aged 51 years, Mary Ann Dudgeon married the Reverend James E MacDougall at Springfield House. The Reverend was minister to the Ladyloan parish church having been ordained in 1851; minister and church were to be united for 49 years. There was no manse attached to this church therefore the couple lived at Springfield House. By all accounts they were a devoted loving couple, quaint and somewhat old fashioned. Mary Ann was unfortunately very deaf and had to use an ear trumpet. Even then, voices had to be raised for her to hear. It was not uncommon for husband and wife to be seen shouting at each other while walking the streets of Arbroath. The town's people of the time respected their conversation but it must have been difficult to ignore.

Although being comfortably well off, James MacDougall was noted for being frugal and thrifty. Albeit Springfield House retained its female household staff and gardeners, it would be supposed that the contents of the house and modern ideas of the time were not a priority to this couple. He was generous to his church and returned his yearly stipend so that maintenance repairs could be made to the church. He and Mary also placed two stained glass memorial windows in the Ladyloan Church; one in memory of her father David Louson, the other to his father. This church was finally demolished in 1967 along with most of the houses and businesses in the Ladyloan area; a sad reflection on this part of the town. I have been unable to find any trace of the stained glass windows having been saved so I must presume they were demolished with the building.

Mary Ann died 3rd June 1885 and was just shy of her 70th birthday. Mary had prepared for this time many years before and her will was straight forward. She left everything to her husband James E MacDougall. All her means and estate, heritable and moveable. Her wish and desire was that he should have the absolute and unlimited use and enjoyment of her whole means. It is an interesting turn of phrase "unlimited use" but when we add the element of 'Trustees' into the mix, it becomes clearer.

When David Louson was making his will over a period of some years, he set up a safeguard system for all his investments. This was a committee of trustees who were the watch-dog of his financial empire. Although Springfield Estate was Mary's, the financial spend on maintenance and capital budgets on the property as with other matters would have been in the hands of the trustees. Although her husband inherited her estate and house, the trustees still held the property in trust. James MacDougall would have remained the titled owner along with enough capital to run the property coming from rents, feus and other investments upheld by the trustees.

James was aged seventy three when his wife died and Mary, in her long years at Springfield House with her father, first husband, on her own and second husband had made the role of 'lady of the house' her own. When she died, this most certainly would have had an impact on the running of the household.

By 1891, David Ruxton Head Gardener had retired and Ian Hadden, the sole domestic servant was approaching retirement. The Trustees saw fit to appoint a gardener and were indeed searching for a house-keeper for James who was now 79 and although in fairly good health, required looking after. This post fell upon Miss Margaret Anderson who, in late 1891 or early 1892 took up the position of Housekeeper at Springfield House. Margaret had excellent references as she had worked for quite a few of the large mansion houses around Arbroath and until recently for James Shanks, Engineer (lawnmower fame) at Rosely House Arbroath as cook and housekeeper. It is probably safe to say that after the death of Mary Ann, Springfield became a rather quiet sleepy place that time almost forgot. The arrival of Margaret Anderson had, I am sure, made a difference to the household but there remained a quiet absence for the house was full of memories.

However, Arbroath had by contrast moved on by the late 1880s. The Council had, by public subscription, purchased farmland bordering Springfield Estate. This was the Braeheads which ran down to the sea and along to the Ness. This was transformed into what is now Victoria Park. It was formally opened with great celebration on 22 June 1897 being the date of Queen Victoria's Diamond Jubilee.

Unfortunately, even in those days, geographically miles from the British capital, London put out the call in 1899 when the Boer War began on October 10th of that year. However Britannia's empire of imperial power was nearly over and the Queen herself died in the January of 1901. That was a year of personal grief also for Mrs Mary Dickson nee Louson, the sister of Mary Ann, for she lost her husband in April 1901 and James Ewan MacDougall died on the 23rd December of that year also. James was 89 years of age and had been feeling justifiably tired of late, his appearance at dinners and church functions had gradually become less and less. In fact he turned down an invitation in the week before he died. Margaret Anderson had been with him at the end and for ten years, had looked after him and managed Springfield House. She had also fulfilled the role of friend and companion and, at 64 years of age must have enjoyed the less strenuous regime in which she may have found herself elsewhere.

James MacDougall was a kind man and well aware of the harsh conditions life handed out to many. His thoughts when writing his will some months before his death must have dwelt on Margaret and her advancing years. It would be difficult for her to find a post that befitted her age and requirements. A gift of a small gratuity would hardly see her through her remaining years and he himself did not have family in need. Perhaps in his thoughts, Mary Ann encouraged him to aid Margaret Anderson and he did so.

James stated that it was his wish that Margaret Anderson be entitled to the income and revenue from the whole residue and estate during her lifetime and that she was entitled to reside in Springfield House and have full use of all furniture and fittings during her lifetime. The rates and taxes related to Springfield House and the expense of keeping up the building, grounds and garden was to be borne out of the entitlement of the income and revenue provided. How well this was received by some people in the community is difficult to know and try they may have done to over-turn this will. Certainly to no avail. It stood. Margaret remained at Springfield House and upheld James' wishes to keep house, garden and grounds in a well maintained manner. There may have been times of loneliness but also of relief. Opportunities to invite friends and remaining family perhaps and to sit on a summer's day, feeling the joy of life and giving thought to the man who had made it possible. Perhaps also remembering her parents and how hard it had been for her mother, alone for many months at a time as her father had been a ship-master. Margaret died at Springfield House aged 80 on the 7th January 1917.

The First World War was raging, the war that was to end all wars. God forbid but we never seem to learn. Thousands upon thousands died, many slaughtered so it was not surprising that the Springfield Estate did not sell when put on the market in October 1917. Life was tangible. The war had touched almost all in one way or another. The remaining trustees saw their work as completed; the Louson family now gone. Mary Duncan Dickson (nee Louson) had died in 1915 at Woodville and her surviving family had settled elsewhere.

The Guide newspaper of the period ran a small piece on Springfield history, the drama had been played out and these words are poignant: - "Through the death of a life-renter the estate recently came on to the market. Springfield was always noted for its fine old trees and it is hoped that the new proprietor will allow as many of them to remain as possible." It is a sad reflection that the writer of this piece referred to Margaret only as a life-renter without a name and that the concern was not for the estate as a whole but for the trees only, beautiful and majestic as they may have been.

Finally after many months, the estate was sold in the spring of 1918 to Mr William Greig, Magunzie House near Arbroath. The farm part of the estate, roughly 25 acres, was already tenanted out and this arrangement continued. However, in the May of 1918, a bond for £1500 in security by Wm Greig was processed to Maud Gardyne Lyon Walker or Hartness, wife of John Benn Hartness residing at 63 Albert Palace Mansions, Battersea Park, London. In other words, Mr Greig rented the house (Springfield) and garden surrounding it i.e. the tree lined drive to Mrs Hartness. The walled garden was tenanted out to a market gardener. A good arrangement which was to last several years in fact to August 1929.

Mr Greig, now of Seaton Arbroath, had decided to sell the property and lands and had mentioned it to Provost Chapel. A special meeting of the Town Council with Provost Chapel, Magistrates and Councillors met on 20 September 1929 to discuss the option to purchase the estate of Springfield which included all the land, approximately 29 acres and buildings at a price of £3000. The proposal was unanimously agreed for the purpose of benefiting the community and the common good of the burgh.

The disposition was dated 23 October 1929 and therefore the lands of Springfield now belonged to the people of Arbroath. Such was the vision of the councillors of the time that this latest acquisition would, jointly, with Victoria Park, make a large green community space for the east end.

No doubt the theory behind this concept was correct at the time for people had much simpler pleasures and values. A stroll in the park on a Sunday afternoon having worked long hours within factory or office walls all week; a game of footie on the grass instead of the street, a chance to natter to people of acquaintance or just to sit on the grass and claim a couple of hours of peace, read a newspaper or a book, it was then just what the doctor ordered.

The farm and walled garden continued to be leased out at this time as a remit was undertaken by the Parks and Recreation Committee as to a new layout. Meanwhile the Council debated what to do with the Mansion house and an on site meeting was held at the end of October 1929. In late November 1929, it was decide to serve notice of termination of tenancy on the farmer and market gardener. However, due to a clause in the farmer's agreement, the termination could only happen when he had found other suitable premises. Considering he was to lose his home as well, the gardener's cottage, it seems only fair that time was on his side. As to the market gardener, he wrote to the council and asked if he could rent the garden for a further year at a rent of £10.00. This was declined. By March/early April, the Parks Department suggested that the garden be put in order for the summer. I found this a little odd considering the park was not yet open to the public, a new layout not yet completed nor presented to the committee. Yet another meeting was arranged in late April 1930 to inspect the walled garden and the question of layout was again raised. It was put to the Burgh Surveyor and Parks to prepare a sketch for the council. In the meantime, the buildings within the wall were to be cleared away, the ground dug and grassed.

Today of course we would throw up our arms in horror at the very thought of turning an old Victorian garden that was still in existence into a walled grassed park, at least without finding out what treasures may still be there. What damage was done at this point is unknown but it is certain that the market gardener had been quick to retain anything he thought valuable. The layout arrived in May and it would seem that, apart from putting in a few shrubs here and there, a few seats and a couple of paths; that concluded the walled garden.

It is now September. The tenant farmer has gone and a further meeting had been arranged, this time regarding the house with a view to considering the best way of utilising the premises. Offers were invited for leasing the house as a tea-room and a tenant living on the premises. December came and went but the submitted offers had failed to be accepted by the council. Therefore in January of 1931, it was suggested that the farmland be used as a nine hole golf course and perhaps a putting green. With this association, it seemed appropriate that the house could be used as a club-house.

It was not until September 1931 that a meeting was held instructing the Burgh Surveyor to submit costs for the following:

1) Demolition of the house
2) To upgrade sanitary arrangements and provide tea room accommodation with perhaps someone on the premises
3) Erect a suitable tea room.

It is unknown where the idea came from regarding demolition of the house but certainly between January and September of 1931, the idea had been planted in the minds of the Parks committee. It was reported in the newspaper of the period that the Parks convener was convinced that the layout of Springfield would be made much easier and more satisfactorily by the demolition of the old property i.e. the mansion house. A further member of this committee remarked that from the very start, he saw that the only thing that could be done with the house was to demolish it.

The recommended minute of a club-house seems to have vanished and having dismissed the tea-room idea some months previously, it was suddenly back on the agenda.

In a meeting in November 1931, an estimate of £250 was put forward to demolish the mansion and make up the ground. This was unanimously recommended by the Parks committee. A letter dated 14 December 1931 was presented to the council in which Mrs Greig of Seaton House, as

President of the Town Improvement Association, requested the council give careful consideration before committing this building for demolition. The Parks Department who appear to have had the lead role in this affair, made it quite clear that it would be very difficult to carry out a scheme which would be of any material advantage to the community.

It was all to no avail as the count was two against demolition and fourteen for and so the motion was carried. Less than three days later, the order was given to the Burgh Surveyor that the property be demolished immediately.

Without doubt, this was not the first mansion of Arbroath to disappear and we are indeed on the edge of others going the same way.

Springfield Park was officially opened on 2nd July 1932.

EPILOGUE

When I was young, seven or eight years old, my Mum and I would walk through Springfield Park on a regular basis. In the winter, we would gather the twigs that the wind had blown down from the tall trees. They were grand for the fire, whether for my grandmother's or our own. In the spring, it was the crows that created the firewood by their nest building.

I never knew about Springfield House or the history of the walled garden. I simply enjoyed the park and its amenities. Over the years, these amenities changed from pitch and putt, rock garden, putting green, band stand, paddling pool and swings; only the walled garden remained much the same.

It was not until much later in my life that I went to college for 'Garden History', an extension to my love of gardening. I was fascinated and wondered if there had been any Victorian gardens in Arbroath that may have been 'lost' as it were.

The 1859 map opened up my eyes to Springfield and what you have read is the result of my research.

Having walked this park many years ago, I feel now that, in some way, we have let it decay. Some of the beautiful old trees which a reporter once lingered over and requested to be kept have now gone. Trees have been planted in abundance but are unmanaged. Eco-systems must be cared for, not left unattended. The concept, the dream, the amenities have all gone. All that remains are a few swings. The toilets are no longer open and the building an eyesore. Vandals spray paint on the walls of the garden and dig up the few remaining plants for reasons unknown. However, that elusive spell of my childhood is still there for me and the footprint of Springfield's history lay sleeping until now. Perhaps we can awaken the pleasure it could give if we took more interest in what, after all, is our park.

The veil closes on those who lived within Springfield. The walled garden remains as the guardian of its history. Perhaps a plaque or an inscribed wooden seat would be appropriate within its walls to David Louson as a token gesture to the man who remained faithful to his love of place and one of the Council's own for 46 years.

Looking up to Springfield House

Walled garden in the 1970s

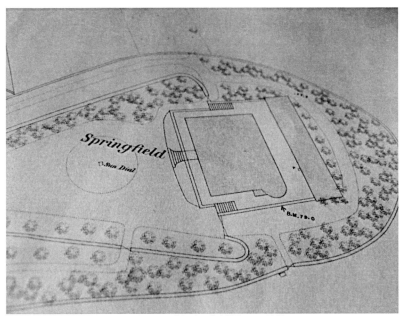

Map layout of Springfield House 1860s
© National Library of Scotland

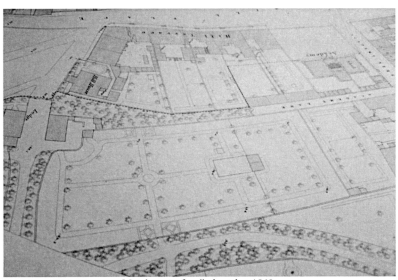

Map layout of walled garden 1860s
©National Library of Scotland

107

PART THREE

SENSE OF PLACE

NOTES ON A SMALL COUNTRY GARDEN
SPRING

With my love for the sea I thought that country living held nothing for me but of course I was wrong. Indeed it did not take long after my parents and I moved from our house by the shore to learn to adore the outside space of garden, fields, woods and verges.

Joy is looking across the field from the garden, watching two hares chasing each other as if playing tig and then suddenly deciding to box each other; no need for gloves or boxing ring here, it's a free for all. I am reminded when, some years ago, our young greyhound, found in a cardboard box at ten weeks, was trying to grab our matriarch mongrel and got a swift swipe of her paw across his nose. She was his surrogate mother and our Alsatian became his Dad.

I am hopeful the newly erected bat and insect boxes will aid the small creatures this coming winter as last, with its prolonged cold spell was disastrous for many shrubs and their inhabitants. Several birds' nests have also been put up and although these may be just used for warmth and resting over the winter, it is a pleasing prospect that a life may be saved.

Gardening is a funny old game if one can call it that. It has a power that captivates you. Unbelievably I hear myself saying in the middle of spring and summer 'I wish it would rain, the garden is desperately needing it.' A contradiction in terms but it has now become an integral part of our lives to care for the plants, birds and animals in what has become literally their garden.

111

What would life be without bees I thought hearing recently of their decline? Farming would be affected greatly, the thoroughly enjoyable honey and most importantly of all listening to the sound of bees on a peaceful summer's evening going from flower to flower, filling their little pockets full of yellow pollen. We noticed the other day that a bee-keeper had put several hives at the edge of the farmer's field not far from us. We are hoping that perhaps these bees will visit.

In preparation of that, where I can I have sown wild flower seed, particularly a bee and butterfly mix. We also intend to leave the dandelions on the verge in front of the house. People passing by will either think we are lazy or crazy but there will be some who will know the reason for bees love dandelions; it is a rich supply of nectar for them. The bright yellow flower-head is made up of roughly 150-200 florets and working as one, they close up in dull weather and at night. Their seed clocks are really works of art, not appreciated as such when we were young however as the idea was to blow the clocks and the number of puffs it took to blow away the seeds would tell you the time. But of course this was helping to disperse the seed parachutes and this can be over one hundred miles distant. We need this plant in our lives because the tap root of the dandelion is used in herbal medicine as it has been for hundreds of years. Not forgetting the butterflies, I have left a patch of nettles and thistles down by the log store for some butterflies such as the tortoiseshell will lay their eggs on stinging nettles. The buddleia is a favourite tree for many butterflies but regrettably, we don't have one in this garden.

Unlike some shrubs and trees that take a life-time to grow, buddleia grows very quickly and requires space and that is at a premium in this garden. But having had a beautiful white buddleia in a previous garden, it is without doubt a mecca for butterflies.

One of the problems of being a detached cottage is that the summer winged insects and birds have no corridor so they do not tend to stay in the garden, only feeding in passing. However seeing them, if only for a few moments, is a privilege. The winter is different for the birds come to get fed specifically because they know the food will be there. That responsibility is rewarding as one never knows what to expect.

Unfortunately all of this creates a problem when one lives in the country, more so now as birds of prey are more common. Having an old holly hedge is a tantalising place for a sparrow hawk and they are masters at sitting quietly; this is the nature of the bird. The little ones are not even aware he is there until suddenly, they are ambushed and in the grip of fierce talons. There is little they or we can do. I have tried placing mesh where I think the hawk may strike, hanging bright reflective CDs on the holly branches but all to no avail. It is the nature of the beast and although we know they also have to eat and feed chicks, our sympathy is with the wee ones. There have been times when luckily one or other of us have spotted him or her waiting almost hidden in the garden and have sent him packing with the noise of a tin whistle and dogs barking excitedly but I have also buried many little broken bodies over the years in the garden.

The blackbirds are long-standing friends, particularly the female who comes right up to the garden door to be fed and then follows me all around the garden. They normally nest in the deep thick broadleaved evergreen bamboo many years old as it gives a lot of protection. This year however they have decided to nest in the pot stand squeezed between several pots I use for summer annuals and a large one for vegetables. Although it is next to the garden shed, my movements back and forth do not appear to concern her. So I will just have to find something else for the plants or do without – well that's me told!'

The robin has disappeared again for the time being anyway. She has gone courting probably so no doubt she will remain in his patch and then return alone to her garden for the winter. They are amazingly territorial.

We are so fortunate to see many different birds in the garden. Many move on such as the blue tits but there a few that linger and some that stay permanently. The blackbirds, yellowhammers, sparrows, a few starlings and other members of the finch family are numerous; all are resident or nest very close by.

The hedge sparrow comes and sits on the window sill, sunning herself and wondering why she cannot reach the plant so close to her. Windows must be so puzzling for birds and animals.

The tiny wren, a mere three and three quarters inches long lives in the hedgerow, difficult to spot as she darts about but she is so very distinctive with her mousy little body, upturned tail and little wings. Along with many other small birds, there are two permanent doves and two partridges that flit in and out and the latest frequent visitor, now named 'Walter', is a cock pheasant.

Freddie the lurcher, although having a wonderful easy going nature and so tolerant of all the other birds, finds Walter just a shade too big and one strut too far. The 'woofs' are however made from inside the porch and the bravo display remains there.

The great spotted (pied) woodpeckers are a star act and their acrobatics to reach the hanging berry or fruit fat never fails to amaze. Last year, the pair brought in their two babies and although it meant more trips to the pet shop for their favourite food, it was well worth it.

The favourite tree in the garden for all the birds is the old rowan. A magical plant in the Highlands of old, it was used for a decoction to cure many ills from sore throats to blood pressure. Today it has a more culinary use for the berries are great for making jelly; that is if there are any left after a visiting flight of field fares. The 'Woody' family however have left their stamp on the old tree with the 'drum' holes all the way up so I fear for the tree as a child with an open wound.

The quiet of the cottage is a great place to hear the greylag geese going over and, on occasions, the lonely sound of a swan calling for its mate. The heron too flies over for we live between two lochs. For a large bird it has the grace of a ballerina particularly on landing and then the outstretch of the wings before folding them so carefully away. The long neck swivels round and he places his head under the wing for a deserved snooze. On awakening, the thoughts will turn to food. He waits silently, watching for any movement by water or field. When satisfied or disturbed, he takes off again; not requiring a runway, all is very effortless. It springs to mind we have still much to learn about aerodynamics.

The days are longer now and the buds are gathering their energy to unfurl into leaf or flower. The name 'April' comes from the Latin 'aperire', a word meaning 'leaf opening'. With sun and April showers, progress is swift and even the perennials have popped their heads above the ground as if not wanting to miss the show. It has after all been a long winter in the dark. There was a time when tulips followed daffodils but now our garden is full of both, flowering as red and yellow sentinels. The wind tries to bend them to its will but some resist by lying almost horizontal. By early evening when the wind has eased, the flowers once more stand to attention in defiance.

We have a family of wood mice, different from the house mouse in that they have large ears and eyes and large back feet, their little chests are white and they have a long tail. They live under the holly hedge and drystane dyke, scampering up and down stealing the bird food. This winter past was so hard, I placed a little feeding station for them under their favourite bit of holly along with a hollow log. We feel so privileged to watch them sitting as they do at the edge of the log, two front feet holding a piece of pink suet, the other mouse holding a large seed, eyes watchful and whiskers quivering. Unfortunately we haven't seen them for a while but then they are mostly active at night and now the cold, cold weather has gone; no doubt they have other things on their mind.

The daylight is fading and twilight descends. I hear the male blackbird doing his rounds of the garden; he is always the last to say goodnight.

Darkness has fallen and the night sky is so full of stars. I remember when I lived and worked in London, it was so rare to see the stars. Having lived with their beauty while growing up only to lose their light midway was devastating; yet later in life to find them again was overwhelmingly beautiful. I recall Longfellow's poem

"Silently one by one, in the infinite meadows of heaven, blossomed the lonely stars, the forget-me-nots of the angels."

It is dawn and other night animals have been in – stoat, weasel, shrew, field vole and perhaps a passing fox. The dogs are out chasing smells, something has been in the garden! But then again it may not be any of these animals. I am reminded of a slogan I saw on a car just the other day which I thought was wonderful: - "A day without fairies is like a day without sunshine." – Who knows!

Pulsatilla

BREAKING IN MY NEW BOOTS

The Scottish hills with their beauty and wildness have always held a special place in my heart. From a very young age, week-end walks with my family were often to the Angus glens of Clova, Glen Doll and Corrie Fee. In the late 1950s, the cattle grid at Braedownie was as far up the glen as you could take your car and so, from there, we would set off armed with wild flower books, binoculars and camera, always with the hope of finding some rare alpine plant high up in the obscure recesses of the crags; perhaps one that Angus botanist George Don had discovered over two centuries before but had since been lost in time. Passing ranks of pine trees, we crossed the South Esk River, the winding track then taking us around the Glendoll Lodge youth hostel before leading us beside the banks of the White Water. The joy then was of perhaps seeing the flash of a dipper in the river's icy flow or looking forward to finding a delicate alpine lady's mantle, tiny saxifrage or even a purple coltsfoot in Corrie Fee. As we headed onwards over the rough track towards either Jock's Road, an ancient hill crossing or into Corrie Fee, I would gaze upwards, hoping to catch the glint of a golden eagle soaring high in the sometimes blue skies above Craig Rennet or beyond the Fee burn's cascading waterfalls. Rain or shine, there were always sights, sounds and scents to enjoy.

Back home on other weekends, I would watch my father getting his battered ex army rucksack out from the cupboard under the stairs, dusting it down before filling it with the essentials required for a couple of nights in the hills while I pestered him with the question of when I too might spend a night in the hills. However, before this could happen, I had to get kitted out with a pair of proper walking boots which meant I had to spend the next few weeks breaking them in - a painful process! Once home from school I would rush around outside, feeding the hens, building carties and generally getting used to these boots that felt far too big. The empty box of sticking plasters in the bathroom told its own story.

My first overnight trip was to be up Glen Clova, spending a night in the Sandy Hillocks hut, so named for its proximity to the hill of Sandy Hillock and then back the next day. Although I had been up the track past the Moulzie, the stalkers cottage, I had never been as far as Bachnagairn before, let alone Sandy Hillocks. It was all very exciting for an eight year old and I felt very grown up indeed as we set off from Braedownie one grey Saturday morning in late May. We followed the River South Esk, crossing the Cald Burn and walking on, the sign to our right pointing up the Capel Mounth, another ancient drovers' track that zigzagged from Glen Doll to Glen Muick near Braemar. Heading onwards past the Moulzie with Cairn Broadlands on our left, a soft drizzle now accompanied us as we made our way to where we hoped to find a bridge across the South Esk. We were in luck that day for in the late 1950s and early 1960s, you could never be sure of getting across the river safely without plunging into the icy and at times fast flowing water; any bridge built usually ended up being swept away at some point in stormy weather. This time, safely across, we were now on the left bank of the river, the Juanjorge looming ahead on our right, its steep sides guarding the entrance to the area called Bachnagairn. By this time, my rucksack felt a ton weight and all I could do was keep hoisting it up my back.   My boots however were broken in and I was almost free from blisters.

At last we crossed the South Esk again this time over the wooden bridge at Bachnagairn, pausing to look at the magnificent water fall before setting off up the twisty and aptly sandy track towards Sandy Hillocks hut.   Soon, we reached the bothy which to my young eyes looked a cold, uninviting, ramshackle place as indeed it was but it was to be home until the following morning.   I spent the night fidgeting between stones that felt like enormous boulders, trying to find a comfortable spot without waking up my slumbering dad and wondering why anyone in their right minds thought this was fun.   But in the early morning I changed my mind as I opened the hut door and stepped outside to see the soft morning light touching the top of Broad Cairn, a Munro of some stature to my left, a small herd of deer grazing peacefully on its slopes and, further round to my right, high above Loch Muick, the magnificent sight of Lochnagar with its brooding dark corries. These sights held me spellbound. The scented air filled my nostrils and flowed through my young body, reviving me and filling me with a sense of awe and happiness. The Scottish hills were teaching me not only to use all my senses but also to give nature the respect it deserves. The sound of a fox barking in thick mist shrouding the hills can be terrifying until you know what it is; the squelch of a peat bog as you helplessly flounder in its sticky midst; the aroma of the beautiful Scots Pine and the sight of an eagle soaring to majestic heights never leave you.

That morning, as I tucked into my breakfast of condensed milk and dried bananas along with a large mug of tea, I knew it wouldn't be long before I set foot in those hills again.

Looking towards the Capel Mounth

BRIEF ENCOUNTER

March is leaving and the infant April is newly born of wind and showers but I feel the wind lighter and the rain comes and goes with a blast of sunlight in between. Like all creatures, I lift my head up to this new found light and rejoice in the radiant April sun.

Snow came late this year February and March, putting the early bulbs and some perennials back but the lovely snowdrops have gone now and the sparrows saw the last of the yellow crocuses; they are wicked little birds at times but I adore them.

Many birds have already built their nests; others are repairing their former apartments. For them it is the time to be in love and we humans are the recipients of recitals and duets that are a sheer joy.

I spotted a hare the other day dancing over the ploughed field in front of the cottage. I thought spring has definitely arrived. When I spotted an early bee, it really did confirm it; quite rightly it was in the sunniest part of the garden.

The potting shed is full and although we have been growing plants from seed for many years, the thrill of seeing a seedling bursting through the compost is beyond words. It is an amazing time-capsule; that this tiny seed has all the genetics and knowledge to grow into such a beautiful flower, shrub, tree or vegetable.

I do not enjoy the sterile flowers nor the hybrid crossbreeding of man's intervention nor his garish colours of the annuals for wild life gets no share and, as more often than not, the flower perfume has been lost. When nature is left to wander and paint the flowers, the dress code is wise and the perfume sublime.

I have had such fortune in the last couple of years to witness newly born voles and so thankful I discovered their nests prior to sinking in a garden spade or fork. What I thought were small holes turned out to be small tunnel runs to a voles nest.

The first one I came across was when I was renewing the ground cover material prior to putting down fresh bark for a small path. There I found a hole about 3 inches by 3 inches and a good 7 or 8 inches in depth. I fell to my knees and peered down. In view was a nest of baby voles a few days old. I put everything back as it was but I knew mum would move them now that I had disturbed things.

The second time this happened was last year. I was dividing perennials when I noticed two or three small tunnels leading under the plants. At first I thought "mouse" but then I realised it was actually using the plant's deep roots to secure the nest. I gently pulled the now loose plant to one side and there was a beautifully made nest of moss and leaves etc. of a vole with three or four naked babies. Again I put everything back and re-established the plants but I rather think, again, Mum would have moved her offspring as soon as my back was turned to a safer haven.

A couple of weeks later, well into April, while admiring the primroses in the border, my eye caught a movement on the edge of the grass. Munching new green leaves were two young bank voles, I believed them to be. I froze momentarily thinking all my birthdays had come at once. Could I possibly retrace my steps and go for the camera! After watching them for a moment or two, I thought it was worth a try. Once in the house and thankful the camera was charged, I turned it to close-up mode, ever hopeful and dashed quietly out again. I did not dare to hope they would still be there but they were – how fortunate was that! I crept down and walked on my knees towards them. One of them dashed off just behind a primrose, not far but the other let me come to within seven or eight inches, looking straight at me as if she did not have a care in the world. She continued to eat her greens and I would swear that little vole had a twinkle in her eye. The other little vole was tempted to come out for he remained watching all the time I was there. As I quietly worked backwards on my knees, I caught sight of Mum hovering in the background, desperate to come to the aid of her baby. This time she need not have worried but unfortunately, she would not have known that. That had been such a privilege and a few moments of pure pleasure. Needless to say, when approaching the spot again a few minutes later, Mum and the young voles had gone.

A CAUTIONARY TALE

Sitting on newly painted fences and gates, on telegraph poles and wires, the swallows announce their arrival back home with joyful exuberance, chattering excitedly about their recent exploits; their glossy steel blue heads and backs with chestnut red foreheads and throats bringing sunlight into our midst. Over the coming days, nest sites are inspected and, once the birds have fully recuperated from their immense overseas journey from Africa, rebuilding begins, recent heavy rainfall helping to provide them with soft mud and grass for the repairs to their nest. It is always an anxious time when weather forecasters announce strong West or North West winds for our swallows' nest sits under the eaves of the cottage's west gable. The ravages of autumn and winter can play havoc with their outdoor homes but soon the repairs are complete and the female is sitting on her nest. Once the eggs are laid, usually four to five but sometimes up to eight in total, both parents take turns at incubation.

At last, the chatter of tiny voices can be heard from on high. Over the next days come rain or shine, the parents constantly feed their hungry brood with a variety of insects including small beetles, many species of flies, moths and flying ants, all caught while the swallow is on the wing. Soon, inquisitive heads appear over the top of the nest, new feathers sticking up on end making the youngsters look like punk rockers. Before long, wings are frantically flapped and stretched followed by amazing acrobatics as the chicks balance precariously on the edge of the nest. Like anxious parents ourselves, we watch every day for any marauder, ready to shout and flap our arms like demented banshees in an effort to frighten the thief away even although swallows are capable and vigorous defenders of their young, unafraid of any predator no matter the size.

Then the day comes when the parents, seeing their offspring are ready to begin the next stage in their lives, change tactics. Swooping in and out of the nest with food in their beaks, the two adult birds don't always feed the hungry youngsters the tasty morsels. Instead, they try to tempt them with the food in an effort to make the chicks leave the nest.

On this particular day, after the morning's tasks and a light lunch were over, it was time for us to get back out to the garden. Without paying any particular attention and thinking the chicks were still safe in their nest, I made my way towards the garden shed. Earlier in the year, we had finally got around to keeping all our garden paraphernalia in one shed in the vain hope of remembering where everything was.

Although the shed door faced north, the west was protected by a fence covered in thick, well established clematis while to the north behind another fence, evergreen trees gave added protection.

As I approached the shed door, I was suddenly dive-bombed by two very irate adult swallows. Retreating rapidly, I just caught a glimpse of four little babies, sitting in a line on the thickest branch of the clematis. While we had been inside the cottage, the four youngsters must have taken the plunge and flown the nest straight into the shelter of the clematis where the parents had very obviously thought we had created the perfect swallow nursery and now I was being told in no uncertain terms that the garden shed was off limits!

For the first few hours, one of the parents was always on duty while the other went for food. Watching from a safe distance, we saw first one and then another of the young swallows as they ventured out of the clematis and on to a metal stand full of garden pots which we realised we would be unable to use for the moment as they had become ideal perching posts! It was wonderful to see their little bodies with barely any tail feathers, baby feathers with just a touch of sheen showing through, their yellow gapes still very pronounced, all chattering away enthusiastically.

Over the following few days, their progress was beautiful to watch. Gradually they learnt to fly out of the nursery and around the garden and then further afield, their anxious and watchful parents always in attendance.

The days of the nursery began to come to an end as the young swallows' feathers grew in taking on a beautiful black sheen and their yellow gapes disappeared. They flew away for longer periods of time although always returning at night to the safety of their clematis nursery. All this time, we were unable to do any gardening for everything from forks, spades, trowels, dibbers, composts, bulbs and lawnmowers were all in the garden shed; we daren't risk going in again in case one of the youngsters arrived back unexpectedly and we frightened them away, perhaps straight into the claws of a waiting predator.

The time was rapidly approaching when they would leave us for good. One evening, having watched them all fly off in the morning, they didn't return. We could only hope they were all safely tucked up somewhere else. The following morning, the nursery was still empty but suddenly, they all appeared again, chattering excitedly as they settled on the garden pots in the nursery. The parents flew in and out, sometimes settling on the clematis with one of the youngsters and resting before flying off again.

This happened for two more days and then they were gone, this time for good. We were filled with both a mixture of sadness at not seeing these beautiful birds again but happiness that the parents had raised four healthy offspring. With the distant deserts increasing in size each year and food shortages both here and overseas becoming greater, we could only hope that one or two might return the following year, repair their nest and rear a new family, filling our clematis nursery once more. Next time however, we will endeavour to get our gardening tools out before that happens.

NOTES ON A SMALL COUNTRY GARDEN
EARLY SUMMER

The spring is melting into early summer and the display of primroses, auriculas, daffodils, tulips, fritillary and the remaining army of spring bulbs are almost over. It is astonishing that already that part of the gardening year has gone and the work of lifting the tulips begins, drying them off and carefully setting them aside for next year. The foliage of the daffs and other bulbs left in the ground is already being lost within the growing perennials. The peony, the blue and red poppies, the iris, delphiniums, the wonderful mix of wild flowers – oh so many, it is good to see them coming up as if meeting old friends again.

This year, after a lapse of some years, I have planted strawberries and raspberries. Five rasp canes just taking up a small space (we moved the picnic table so lunch is a 'knee' job now) and five strawberries in a grow-bag. There does seem to be a big push on to 'grow your own' and having been dissatisfied of late regarding some bought fruit and vegetables, it is a case of 'get on with it then' – time will tell!

I was delighted to catch a glimpse of the mouse family the other day and guess what – two tiny, tiny babies. I wish I could capture a photograph but they are so quick and I have no wish to frighten them in any way.

Having accepted I would probably never see a thrush in the garden, conditions for them not being ideal, I could hardly believe it but there she was, totally absorbed with the task of feeding, obviously very hungry. She remained for three days constantly eating and then she was gone. My wish had been granted and these lovely moments of her life had been shared with mine. She had left a gap in her going but that same day, a blackbird flew in that was surprisingly different. She was white and black and it seemed appropriate to call her 'white princess'. With many blackbirds already in the garden, she took some hassle from the others but she held her own. A week later, she was gone. In my mind I wished her well and hoped she had found a partner to share her life and a garden that would feed and care for them.

Walter the pheasant has injured his foot poor chap but he is still eating us out of house and home. He is obviously camping in the field over the drystane dyke, filled with oil seed rape, an expectancy of a brilliant sea of yellow and tall enough to hide quite a few creatures. We will keep an eye on him and hope his damaged foot is only temporary.

The pied wagtails have popped in, telling us that they are back and nesting nearby and to keep the food and water coming because there are little ones on the way.

The sparrows have already presented their off-spring and there is a great deal of importance with the parents showing them off. However, like the garden itself, it appears that the birds are later with their fledglings, perhaps up to three weeks but it's all go now and some of the parents are looking pretty exhausted.

Remember the blackbird and her nest building on the pot stand? Well unfortunately just after writing that, we found her lovely speckled blue/green eggs on the ground below her nest. It was so sad, something had got to them but it really was a very unsuitable place and easy prey. It may be they are very young and a little undecided for since that incident, they have frantically built several nests within the garden and possibly one at the farm nearby. We suspect that is where the pair is at this time for although the male is feeding here in the garden, he is carrying food over towards the farm. It is strange not hearing his song and it is so missed.

I rose early this morning before the sun's rays were too strong. It was soothingly quiet. The dew had been heavy and was still held in some of the flower cups; the trees and shrubs whispering in delight that they are free of wild wind so they may show their flowers to perfection. The grass is sparkling with diamond droplets which hopefully will aid its roots to regenerate. Having dogs, it gets a fair pounding and the demand on it is high. Grass patching is an on-going occupation but it is all worth the effort.

Our greyhound loves to sunbathe and expects his blanket to get moved around with the sun. It looks strange but absolutely necessary that he gets his pet sun-block on particularly his ears; being fair he burns if not. He is hauled in very reluctantly after a bit as he might get sun stroke. What a dog! The other dogs have more sense, lying under shady trees, trying to catch flies. Freddie chases bees and wasps and is being constantly told not to as she will, at some point, get stung.

Mum starling has brought her three babies in to feed; they are such good mothers. It is sad that their numbers are down. I know they are noisy and they squabble but they are so entertaining. Apart from the twitters and clicks, they mimic many of the calls of other birds and humans as well, wolf whistles and telephones to name but two. They waddle about the grass picking up insect grubs, looking lovely in their glossy black metallic coats reflecting purple, green and blue. I buried a Siskin today; beautiful birds. I don't know why it died. Sometimes the finch parents bring their offspring in knowing that it has something wrong with it. In previous years we did have an outbreak of 'Trichomonsis', a parasite-induced disease among the finches. They appear very puffed up and not able to drink or eat. We kept washing their feeding stations and drinking facilities but many succumbed. Luckily this year we have not had a single case that we know of and the little siskin did not die from that disease.

We are lucky for we have six or seven yellow hammers here on a regular basis, yet another bird that the numbers are down and it is on the red alarm list. It is yellow as the name implies with a darkish rump, an exotic looking bird. They do not nest in the garden preferring a large gorse bush, sanctuary against predators, but they do come in to feed most of the year.

Sitting by the window on a warm but grey day in late May, I was entertained by a dunnock (hedge sparrow) and her three babies. They differ from other sparrows by their colouring and nervous gait, brown with a rufous tinge while streaked with greyish white. No sign of the male but she managed perfectly, babies trailing in her wake, feeding them one by one. It was heart-warming to see for they too are on an amber warning list.

I feel we need the peace and quiet, away from the violence of life even more today and the rush to get here and there is without real importance. In the country, that rush comes at a price for I have buried many pussies found run over outside our gate. Not ours for we learnt our lesson early on. There is a baby fox buried here in the garden with the same fate and only yesterday, we met with two young deer 200 metres apart lying on the verge. They too had met their deaths by vehicles. Ours is not a main road, no buses or heavy lorries come except farm vehicles and they, to be fair, drive fairly slowly. It is cars, vans and motor bikes driving at break-neck speed, 70 to 80 miles per hour. What I cannot understand is why come this way if not to see the beauty around you and at that speed, you quite literally see nothing. Scattered everywhere on country roads are the remains of young crows, rabbits, hares, deer and pheasants etc. – what price a life unless it is your own.

I grow 'comfrey' by the hedge, a plant of about four feet in height. It enjoys wet ground and, as the cottage's rainwater downpipe runs into terracotta drains, the comfrey enjoys the benefit of this arrangement. Bumble bees so enjoy its nectar so it is worth growing just for that. This plant has a history for medieval monks used it as poultices for broken bones. I use it by cutting a little of it down later in the year, soaking it in water for some weeks then bottling the juice and bingo, I have wonderful liquid fertiliser for the following year (diluted of course).

Despite the fact that there is no pond in the garden, I have seen adult dragon flies here. The dragon fly has a two year aquatic life and then only lives a further month as an adult. For some reason they are attracted to an old conifer in the garden and with an old tale that a well was here about and with living between lochs, it is perhaps a possible explanation. The wings glisten in the sun and a dragonfly has this ethereal body of green and blue. As a species they go away back in time and can been seen in fossils. In its millions of years, it has learnt well and can fly over fifty miles an hour, fly sideways and even backwards. How clever is that?

It is gloaming now for in the summer it never really gets totally dark. Shadows appear, bats, tiny flying mammals much misunderstood. Their ultrasonic hearing probably the most accurate in the world; perhaps it is to compensate for their very poor vision. They detect the exact position of an insect and do not get lost in the countryside. These attractive creatures need our help for we have reduced their numbers by reducing their insects

The yearly painting starts soon in between rainy days and windy ones. Fences, log store and workshop combined garden shed all require upkeep from the elements. It feels at times like the Forth Rail Bridge having just finished only to start again. We won't be able to say that phrase now that a 10 year special paint has been used on the bridge. I wonder if we can get some of that!

We have three bird baths for the birds; two smaller ones for them to drink and a large one for bathing. We were fortunate for my father was a stone-mason and carved them out of red sandstone many years ago for his own garden. When my parents died, it was a joy to have the carvings for both sentimental and functional reasons. The stones have moved house many times and continue to give pleasure. It is just great to watch the birds' line up for their baths. There are squabbles of course and great flapping of wings with the bath constantly requiring topping up but no wonder the Corydalis flexiosa, a plant originally from China with gorgeous blue flowers does so well, tucked under the side of the plinth of the bathing stone with water being continually sprayed on to its leaves. On sunny days, it's a case of a straight line of smallish mixed birds sitting with wings outstretched like a clothes line drying the washing.

I think it is this communion of living with nature that makes the country so enjoyable. For me, nature is a true leveller. To love it is all consuming. It is of course what you make it but given a chance, the plants and wild life will make it for you.

Baby mouse

THE STONE BENEATH OUR FEET

There are no voices, no sound of horse's hooves, no echo of breaking rocks and you will listen in vain for the sound of the little Carmyllie Pilot, the small steam train, nor will you hear the turning of the windmills. The land is quiet now except for birdsong.

As I drive along this age old road, I always have the feeling that I am moving backwards in time for I am surrounded in this landscape by stratified rock and the feeling reflected is primeval.

I drive through the villages of Carmyllie and Redford a mere two or three miles and yet the harvest of a by-gone era bears witness to at least a dozen quarries. In this Angus county there are many more, the quality of the stone varying. However the Carmyllie parish quarries yielded the best quality of stone for roofing slates and pavements. The stone is hard but has the ability to lend itself to being split into flat slabs, thus perfect for slates, flooring and pavement.

A Geologist's knowledge of time is different from the lay-man's. Our thinking of old and ancient is by comparison very modern. They class these 'lower red sandstone' rocks, the 'Devonian Period' at an age that takes your breath away, 400 million years or so. The creation of the rock was not instant; many many millions of years would have been required to create our 'pavement'. Their very make up was of a violent birth at a time of volcanic eruptions, lava flows and many flowing rivers. This land of ours was warmed by a hot sun and surrounded by tropical seas for we sat at the equator then. Many fossils are to be found in the quarried stones telling us the story of our land's tropical adventures.

This lower old red and grey sandstone runs approximately from the Carse of Gowrie in Perthshire to the mouth of the River Lunan in Angus. It is along the top of this arch that the Carmyllie parish rocks occur and are among the oldest rocks in the district. The name 'Carmyllie' is itself probably of Celtic origin meaning a 'high rocky and bare place'. I have no doubt in the 18th and 19th centuries that name suited it very well.

The early centuries of quarrying would have been by hand and assisted later by windmills, the main activity was cutting heavy rough slates about one inch thick. These were taken by horse and cart to Arbroath and sent by ship to various cities and towns Glasgow, Edinburgh, Dundee, Aberdeen, Liverpool, London and so on. Although there was a small amount of paving produced by the quarries at this time, this was heavy and exhausting work for these paving stones could be any size and up to fourteen inches thick. By this time also, it was necessary to dig deeper for the seams of rock required for pavement. The 'pavement' was delivered by horse and cart to Arbroath harbour 5 miles distant and so it became known as 'The Arbroath Pavement'; consequently many streets in Arbroath were paved in this wonderful stone.

The heavy work took its toll for many quarrymen and stonemasons suffered dust inhalation causing silicosis of the lungs. By good fortune, a great aid was forthcoming to this industry and gave it the boost it needed to progress.

James Hunter of the Parish invented various machines to aid the quarrying industry, stone planing machines in 1834 and later his son George invented the stone saw and indeed carried on making improvements to the dressing machinery.

The windmills were replaced by engines with lifting hoists attached. Progress indeed but unfortunately, as always, there is a down side. James and his son George were relatively poor as they gained little recognition nationally. However the machines were used at Carmyllie and throughout Angus replacing manual labour.

Along with the now increased production, there came the railway for it was the only means of transporting the stone pavements in any large quantity. The main Dundee to Arbroath line was extended by a branch line to Redford in 1855. From there small track lines ran to the quarries. A steam power crane lifted the stone pavements, ornamental carvings, balustrades, pillars, steps, lintels etc into the waiting train wagons. Once at Redford, they were taken to Elliot station and on to various destinations throughout Britain. As was the fashion at this time, many large businesses, banks etc were indebted to this Carmyllie stone for their polished floors. Perth railway station is another example as indeed is the Forth Road Bridge, its piers held fast by Carmyllie stone. They were also taken to other ports and from there, travelled abroad to South America, USA, Australia and Europe to name but a few.

The industry was at its peak about 1870 and survived over a period of nearly seventy years, finally ending at the beginning of the 2nd World War. One or two of the quarries remain open not now in large scale production but the stone is still required for restoration purposes for many large houses, mansions and palaces etc. throughout Britain and beyond.

However it is to some of the ecclesiastical buildings where these pavements dwell that I pay homage. Walk within the walls of Glasgow Cathedral, York or Westminster, Cologne Cathedral and many more of the great cathedrals of Europe and possibly a cathedral near you. When you walk or kneel if that is your way, remember this stone now worn by touch, came from a humble and small community that possibly you have never heard of but these people of Carmyllie parish were proud of what they achieved and we today should remember them with a smile and an acknowledgment that the stone pavement will outlive us all.

NATURE'S BOUNTY

In contrast with my co-author, I grew up in the countryside and was surrounded from a very early age by nature in all its wonderful guises. The local estate that bounded the bottom of our garden was part of my extended playground and throughout all the seasons, I made full use of it all. A great deal of time was spent down by the burn, watching and listening to the crystal clear waters meandering through the mixed woodland. At various periods in the burn's life, there had been an assortment of rickety wooden bridges spanning its girth but for a young child, crossing these bridges was not nearly as exciting as jumping from stone to wobbly stone trying to reach the other side without getting a severe "drooking"!

The burn also heralded other attractions; the distinctive blue and orange flash of a passing kingfisher or the white throat and red breast of a dipper, bobbing up and down on the rocks, cocking its head before disappearing silently into the clear waters in search of food among the myriad of treasures lying in the tinkling water. A jay squawking noisily would interrupt the peace, a shy woodland bird more often heard than seen. If I was very lucky, I caught the rare but mesmerising glimpse of a woodcock; its whispering wing beat the only sound as it flew out of sight; its rest having been interrupted as I made my way through deep piles of crunchy fallen leaves from previous seasons.

Spring would announce itself with canopies of wood anemones followed by banks of creamy yellow primroses while willow trees dipped their sinewy tendrils into the burn. Beech, elder, rowan, oak and ash trees all showed off their new leaves and willow warblers arrived, their liquid song filling the air with the promise of warm days. Swallows would swoop into our garage to reclaim nests from previous years and hares would meander across fields full of green shoots of wheat and barley growing in regimented rows. Wood pigeons or "cushie doos" would set up home in the rhododendron hedge surrounding the house, not entirely a welcome addition when vegetables had been planted in the garden. Nothing ever seemed to deter them in their quest for titbits. They paid no heed at all to the old cardigans and hats stuck on poles among the crops, supposedly to scare them off.

As spring grew into summer, curlews with their alluring call continued about their business, prodding the ground for worms with their long curved bills while peewits or lapwings put on marvellous displays of flight, calling incessantly often right through the night. If caught unawares, the frightening laughter of the 'yaffle' bird or green woodpecker, watching from a safe distance out of sight from prying eyes, made the hairs on the back of your neck stand up on end but if you were lucky enough to spot this beautiful bird, its distinctive markings were wonderful to behold with its bright green rump and red on the top of the head.

Summer flowed on towards autumn; fungi appeared and among the many edible varieties, field mushrooms abounded, some so big a family of field mice could picnic beneath a single mushroom cap quite safely. With the local farmer's permission, baskets would be filled to the brim always with the proviso of taking only what was required while not only leaving plenty for others but enough for the spores to sink back into the ground and hopefully rise again the following year. Once picked, the mushrooms would be taken home and turned into delicious meals; sliced and fried in butter then served on hot toast or stuffed and baked in the oven. Made into soup they made a substantial lunch-time treat or for supper, a thick buttery omelette and if there were any mushrooms left, they were dried for winter consumption.

Then there were wild strawberries usually eaten on the spot; tiny little red jewels that tasted so sweet and brambles which, in a good year, could be turned into jam or bramble crumble. Both fruits were always sampled fully before being brought home, hands and lips stained purple by the juices giving testament to that!

Back down in the woods, the green leaves of the splendid trees were turning into wonderful russets, reds and oranges. Acorns fell from the oaks, ash keys flittered to the ground; elder and rowan berries ripened to deep purples and reds awaiting the attentions of mistle thrush and blackbird to gorge themselves before dispensing the seed to other parts of the woods for new growth to begin the following year. Fallen tree branches were sawn up into manageable sizes and carried shoulder high up to the garage to be stacked along with masses of kindling all gathered in preparation for the winter. Leaf mould was painstakingly sieved into wheelbarrows for mulching the garden, while red squirrels were too busy gathering in their own winter supplies to bother about two legged creatures. Field mice began the process of building their winter hidey-holes in hay-stacks while pheasants strutted around the fields, gorging on the fallen seeds of the gathered crops.

Autumn grew into winter and slowly the countryside settled down into quiet slumber. These memories are never far away and the thought that we are losing so many of these birds, animals and plants is a sad reflection of our time.

NOTES ON A SMALL COUNTRY GARDEN
AUTUMN

The beginning of autumn; the season of rustic hues, early morning frost, cold bright days and lengthening shadows.

My lady the birch tree has now dressed for the Autumnal season and she looks beautiful in artists' colours of orange, bronze and yellow. Alongside her is the Japanese Acer, his leaves the colour of vermilion. What a pair they make and yet, slightly further down the garden is the climbing rose 'Leaping Salmon', holding on to its last rose of summer.

Gardens are far from empty at this time. The chrysanthemum, the ice-plant, Japanese anemones, begonias, primroses are all determined to carry on for as long as possible. I am proud of them all. However I must give high praise to the perennial wallflower, flowering in May and still showing her colours in late autumn.

Wild red poppies are standing to attention at the garden gate. How appropriate as we approach Remembrance Sunday.

I am on my way to fill up the bird bath for the third time and it is not yet midday. The holly hedge is a mass of sparrows awaiting baths and feeding time (three times a day). The noise is deafening as I pass the hedge. A few fly out just missing my head and land on the bamboo. The sparrows are so light; the bamboo branches hardly register their weight. The blue tits are back for the winter, flying in to the garden in groups. I used to think that these same tits stayed in the garden or roundabout but of course they don't;

they move on and it is different blue tits nearly every day. Hundreds and hundreds will pass through the garden – it is magical, isn't it. The other day, my attention was drawn to the rear window of the cottage. A blue tit was navigating round the whole of the window making quite a din. He was obviously looking for beasties which he seemed to be getting. On inspection later, I realised he had also been pecking the window mastic, a row of little beak marks clearly visible.

I haven't seen Walter the pheasant since late summer. Last time I saw him, his damaged foot appeared to be somewhat better for although walking with a slight limp, he was stomping around the garden, feeding and preening as good as new. Of course I take seeing pheasants for granted living in the country but living in a city, they would be a much rarer sight. They are originally a native of Southern Asia. The Romans, blamed for everything good or bad, are earmarked for having brought the pheasant over to England. It is a fact however that it is mentioned in 11th century literature. The male is a colourful bird, brown, orange and black, his neck a metallic green with white markings. The female as usual in nature a dull colour by comparison, a sandy colour with shades of darker brown. I like to think she is that colour because she blends in better with natures colours. Being a good mother with many babies to look after, possibly ten or so for 10 months or more, she needs to feel nature's protection.

Robbie is back but I say that with less assurance that it is the same bird that left the garden some months ago. She follows you around the garden, hopeful that you will dig up worms for her. The Robin's song is so endearing to us but she is really singing to let other robins know she is here and to keep away from this garden for she is its guardian.

The log man is coming today with a ton of sustainable logs, the first of the season. It is good that it is a dry day. We will get them stacked into the log store. Tonight the stove will burn bright and welcoming with logs stacked up by the fire. The dogs love the fire almost as much as they do going out.

We are too far into the country to have children visit for Halloween (guising) but we share their enjoyment by watching the official firework display from the garden, albeit we are a few miles from the bonfire site. Some of the fireworks these days are really spectacular.

I was awoken somewhat early the other morning to a loud drilling sound from the garden. The light wasn't very good but I could make out 'Woody' the woodpecker on the clothes pole hammering away at it despite the fact that suet balls and nuts were hanging close-by. The woody family successfully raised two chicks this summer; by their colouring a male and a female. They were brought into the garden by Mum and Dad initially. Dad was clearly teaching his boy how to balance on the hanging suet and nut box. After fifteen or twenty minutes, he gave up and flew off obviously in disgust. The young woodpecker was left holding on to the suet ball with one foot and the nut box with the other while trying to peck at a starling as he tried to land on another suet fat alongside. Thankfully the young pair has got the right idea now and come and go to the garden to feed.

It is the season for fungi and when out walking the dogs in the woods, it gives much pleasure in trying to identify the species although I personally never pick what I see, not knowing enough about what is good or bad. There are a few fungi species that appear in the garden. From the billions of spores that are released at fruiting time, it is hardly surprising that a few land on fertile soil. I spotted the lovely orange "Staghorn" variety in the rockery. It is just like stags horns in miniature. The other common fungi that visits the garden is the Sulphur tuft, yellow clumps attached to the base of old trees. They change colour as they age to a grey-violet. It can however be mistaken for Honey fungus which will kill a tree, spreading under the soil and under the tree's bark. Apparently when the caps are cooked, this fungus is edible – needless to say I haven't tried it!

The mouse family have gone, to my disappointment. At least I haven't seen them for some months. Possibly they are still about although by now it is a new generation, collecting fallen nuts, rose hips etc. on their nightly patrols. So early dark now but as yet, few nights of really heavy frost. I hope they have settled in for the winter to come and their store of food carries them through.

I have noticed in the garden for the last couple of years the lack of ladybirds. This follows perhaps on the lack of aphids. The ladybird lays her eggs on plants overrun with aphids, food on tap as it were but they too are down in numbers. Like the children, my favourite ladybird is the red one with seven spots. This colour is a warning to birds that they are not good to eat. Having spoken about the ladybird, another insect that is absent this year is the earwig, usually plentiful but noticeable by its drop in numbers. Looking fierce with its pincers, it is harmless to humans. They hide during the day in crevices, gate hinges etc., active at night, eating leaves and flower heads. Chrysanthemums and dahlias are the favourite flowers. They also enjoy fallen fruit. I say fallen but they can actually fly; they just cannot be bothered to do so. Mum earwig has her babies in October and cares for them all through the winter. Perhaps it is not just the bees that are disappearing.

Autumn has much to recommend it for all around the colours are so beautiful but if I had to choose a further wonderful and mysterious happening in autumn, it would be the crows. They gather in the gloaming time with the remains of an orange and red sky. They lift in unison from the tall fir trees one hundred yards from the cottage, their movements and call are as one. They fly in silhouette in a circle of up to half a mile landing back in the fir trees only to take off again almost immediately. Round they go the sky slightly darker now. They finally land and settle for the night in the high fir trees. The air is silent and the light fails. The cottage lights create eerie shadows.

Autumn, the season steeped in mists and tranquillity. The time of abundance with fruit, berries, fungi and nuts; nature's way to assist the wild creatures through the winter. The grey and brown of the landscape is in evidence now. The trees have done their best to hold on to their colours of umber, yellow and brown but they must rest and it is their last gift to us; to gather their leaves and return them to the earth as leaf-mould, to a gardener more precious than gold.

Dandelion clock

A MOMENT IN TIME

On a cold morning in early February with a view to the Angus hills, a watery sun pushing through plumes of grey clouds, the sky lark, a little crested bird soars almost vertically towards the heavens, then hovers on high before plummeting straight down again, all the while singing its joyous song for everyone to hear. It is heralding a new spring.

Throughout February and March as snowdrops and crocus push through the cold hard earth lighting up even the darkest corner, the sky lark continues its cheerful song in the skies above. So high in the sky does it fly it becomes almost invisible to the naked eye, yet still the magical song effortlessly floats down to enrapture those below. Even although severe frosts and snow may linger, the sky lark continues to proclaim each day with its song of unbroken beauty.

By the end of March, its nest on the ground at the edges of fields and moors and lined with soft grass will be ready for its first brood. As the female incubates the eggs, the male proudly continues to sing, bringing in constant supplies of moths, flies, aphides and seeds. Occasionally, the lark can be seen sitting among clods of earth or on top of a hedge while searching for food, its crest proudly displayed.

In April, as the sky lark's first brood is hatching, the woodlands start to burst forth and soon, the rippling sweet unmistakeable song of the willow warbler can be heard. As carpets of anemones followed by delicate creamy yellow primroses fill the ground, from up above in the canopies of lime green beech leaves, the willow warbler flits. Its restless flight takes it from majestic oak to whispering birch, rowans and elders in its quest for insects and spiders.

Late April and into May sees the willow warbler making its nest at the bottom of hedges or on banks, sometimes among ivy clad walls. The nest is built with moss woven with grass then lined for warmth with feathers.

Throughout the late spring and the summer months, the willow warbler's fluid song is often the only indication of where this secretive bird is. Although called a willow warbler, it has no great preference for willow trees and can be heard in well-timbered and bushy places, even in large wooded gardens, its melodious song a joy for all to hear.

By late summer, both birds become quieter and as the fields and woodlands settle into autumn and early winter approaches, they fly to warmer climates, leaving us with only a memory of their wonderful song.

THE FLOWER OF THE GODS

Dianthus deltoides is better known perhaps as the 'Maiden Pink'; a member of the Pink family 'Caryophyllaceae'. This beautiful small plant grew wild in many parts of Britain and not more so than the cliffs east of Arbroath at the 'Redhead', about a mile from the old historic mansion house of Ethie.

These cliffs and onwards to Arbroath were a haven to many interesting wild flowers and all appeared to be plentiful in the late 19th century. 'The Flora of Arbroath and its Neighbourhood' published in 1882 and written by the Arbroath Horticultural and Natural History Association states that "Dianthus deltoides was frequently found at the east cliffs of Arbroath."

Also, William Gardiner (1808-1852), a Dundonian who pursued botany for the love of it, for its own sake and certainly not to make money, was captivated by the Maiden Pink growing on the summit of the 'Redhead' and so impressed was he that he wrote a poem to this beautiful flower.

> "Upon the Redhead's dizzy brink
> The Maiden Pink doth take her stand.
> Like some fair nymph, whose ardent eye
> Looks forth upon the ocean bland."

The flowers of the Maiden Pink have toothed petals which are pink and are distinguished by a darker band of red around the centre, sometimes looking like dots. The leaves are a greenish-blue with a bluish bloom. It favours dry sandy banks and rock crevices. They love the sun and close their petals on dark days and when night approaches.

The wild pinks are the most noble of flowers and even their name 'Dianthus' captivates the imagination. The original wild Dianthus Caryophyllus was a native of Southern Europe and its Greek name 'Dianthus' means Dios – divine and Anthos – flower and is known as the Flower of Zeus.

Although this plant was beautiful, all favoured plants of the period were not. They did not have to be because, unlike today, the scent of the flower or the medicinal purpose was much more important than the look of the flower itself. This flower family gave the Romans the dried cloves which they used in their wine and that may well be the connection of this plant from Europe. As with many other things, it is possible the Romans brought the seed over to Britain and it flourished.

It is difficult to gain an accurate history of plants; many had their written beginnings in the 16th century but had been growing wild long before then. It is with regret that today, when you walk the cliff headlands, you cannot see this 'flower of the Gods' for it has gone. In innocence, many plants will have had their flowers picked before seed; others dug up and transported to rock gardens. Some battled wind, rain and sea spray before giving up the fight.

So, in some respects, we must be thankful to people like William Gardiner. Having said that, many early botanists did not understand the concept of taking a little seed and perhaps one or two specimens. Many hundreds of actual plants in the wild were taken to send all over the country to different organisations. The botanists were paid for these thus made their living this way. It is sad however to realise just how many of our wild plants have gone and that our coastal walks or country lanes will never be the same.

"Then, Maiden Pink thou teachest us
   That joys in prospect may deceive us
   Till time his passport hath bestowed
   To that bright land where nought shall grieve us."

THREE LOCHS AND A BASIN

On a crisp spring morning before the wind comes out to play, the waters of the Loch of Kinnordy near Kirriemuir are still and calm. The only ripples breaking the surface come from breakfasting ducks diving down for another tasty morsel within the loch's depths. Swans glide elegantly across the loch clearly unperturbed by a flock of exuberant oyster catchers shrilly calling above them. The reed beds, home to sedge warblers and reed buntings in later months stir and rustle as ducks stealthily move within them. Out on the loch, floating bog bean thrives. Between May and July, its feathery star-like flowers are pollinated by bees and butterflies and although the flower scent is unpleasant, this medicinal plant is attractive to beetles and flies, ideal for an inland loch with its varied inhabitants. At the Loch of Kinnordy, the RSPB have created bog bean islands, carefully reducing their size in order to create ideal nesting sites for the black-headed gull. Although called black-headed, these boisterous, acrobatic birds for most of the year have white heads but in the breeding season, their heads turn a rich chocolate brown which, from a distance, look black. These same bog bean islands are also perfect breeding sites for the rare black-necked grebe, a gorgeous bird with golden chestnut tufts of feathers on its face in the breeding season. As both of these birds are on amber alert, it is good to see how much is being done to provide a safe haven for them at the loch. There is something restful about sitting in one of the hides, the window open; the willows gently waving and rustling in the cool breeze. Throughout the seasons there is an abundance of nature to be seen and heard. Greenshank, redshank, wigeon, mallard, shoveller, smew, teal and curlew to name but a few busily feed in the rich water. The loch has also attracted the attention of a bittern, a scarce secretive bird that may occasionally be seen fishing in the reed beds. In the spring, the booming of the male may be heard, its distinctive call resounding around the water of the loch. Great spotted woodpeckers drum relentlessly into nearby trees and red squirrels run up and down the tree trunks, jumping with ease and grace from branch to branch, tree to tree. Yellowhammers, goldcrests and treecreepers join in while the wonderful and at times comical brown hare relishes this safe environment away from the fear of the gun. Osprey dive into the water for a juicy bite; marsh harriers plunder and pillage where they can while dragonflies skim across the loch's surface. The rich vegetation at the side of the loch, home to water vole and otter has another inmate; Koniks, a species of hardy pony that feed on the rough vegetation and wet ground. These tough ponies help improve the ground and benefit breeding waders such as lapwings, yet another bird now on the RSPBs red alert list.

Nature hasn't been the only occupant of this tranquil setting for back in the 18th century when the loch was being drained for the marl, limy clay used as manure, a crannog was revealed. Crannogs were some of the oldest loch dwellings found not only in Scotland but also in Ireland and Wales. They were mainly timber roundhouses supported on piles driven into the loch bed no doubt forming a safe sanctuary for the inhabitants although if wood was difficult to find, rock was piled into the loch to form an island and a stone building erected. According to Alan Reid in his book of 1909 called "The Regality of Kirriemuir", the Loch of

Kinnordy was a mile in length and about half a mile wide, full of pike, perch, eel and in its midst was a large group of stones on top of which a house or fort had been built although very little was visible. The stones that could be seen appeared to be regular, almost in a circle, fixed in the water with trees as planks of oak, some of which were still remaining.

Around 1820, an oak logboat was discovered while marl digging was again being carried out near to the crannog. The boat was recorded by Sir Charles Lyell, an eminent geologist and was said to be 15 foot in length and 3 foot wide. The boat was analysed and assumed to be of prehistoric date. Apparently the boat has since been radiocarbon-dated to around 791 to 801AD. The fragmented remains are in the safe keeping of Dundee's Special Collections Unit but unfortunately, due to its fragile condition, it cannot be viewed. Mr Reid also mentioned in his book that there was an old site of a village of wattle huts situated just above the crannog but no trace of this has ever been found. However, one other find that was made in the 19th century was that of an Auroch's skull. Aurochs were ancient ox like beasts that stood six foot tall at the shoulder and roamed Britain more than 7,500 years ago becoming extinct around 4000 years ago. This almost complete skull is on display at the McManus Art Gallery and Museum in Dundee.

The Loch of Kinnordy is easy to find being around two kilometres from the town of Kirriemuir. Kirrie, as it is known locally, is possibly best known for three things – being the gateway to the Angus glens of Clova, Prosen and Isla; the birthplace of J M Barrie creator of Peter Pan and where Kirriemuir gingerbread was invented by Walter Burnett. No walk around the loch would be complete without some of this delicious sticky treat, best served with lashings of butter.

The county of Angus is fortunate in having numerous lochs and wildlife reserves. To the east of Kirriemuir, the lochs of Rescobie and Balgavies offer yet more plentiful opportunities to sit and watch nature in all its forms. Rescobie loch sits on the right hand side of the B9113 Forfar to Montrose road and is well worth a detour. When the Rescobie Loch Development Association formed in the 1960s to provide loch fishing, perch and pike ruled the waters. The RLDA successfully removed those voracious feeders, restocking the loch with rainbow and brown trout. For those who love fly fishing, this loch is a treat. At around 200 acres, it has a new boathouse and a welcoming car park where it is easy to spend a leisurely hour sitting at the side of the loch watching the fishermen patiently casting their lines into the waters while ducks swim and dive all around, man and bird giving each other respect in their own way.

East of Rescobie Loch lies picturesque Balgavies Loch. Run by the Scottish Wildlife Trust, it is an intimate loch. Tucked off the Forfar to Friockheim road, the SWTs hide is well situated to see the best of all the loch's inhabitants and as an added bonus, the SWT have made a path around the loch. It is a delightful walk and providing dogs are kept on the lead, they too can enjoy the wonders of this little loch. On the north side, the track takes you along the old Forfar to Arbroath railway line. The remnants of the Auldbar Road station are visible showing it to have been quite a substantial station in its day. It is interesting to note too that back in the 18th century, the town councils of Arbroath and Forfar thought about forming a canal between Arbroath and Forfar to be named the Strathmore Canal. The canal would possibly have been made using the Lunan Water which comes from the lochs travelling east to the sea.

The first survey for this proposal was carried out in 1783 and again in 1817 when Robert Stevenson, engineer of the Bell Rock Lighthouse made another survey. The reason for the proposed canal was the prohibitive cost of taking coal, which was much needed in Strathmore due to the lack of peat, from Arbroath to Forfar via the road. It was even talked about extending the canal to Coupar Angus in the west and Brechin in the north west. If coal could be carried by canal, the cost would be halved. However by 1825 Mr Stevenson proposed forming a railway from Arbroath through Strathmore and regrettably the canal scheme was shelved. Auldbar Road railway station opened in 1838 with the station house being built by the end of 1840. Auldbar Road survived as a thriving station for over 100 years, closing in 1956 although the line remained open until 1965/67. Walking along part of the disused railway line now, it would have been wonderful if the canal had been built or Dr Beeching's axe had not been allowed to fall, causing the demise of this line and countless others; an economic disaster for the whole country.

At first glance, there may not be much going on at the loch but on closer inspection, it is a cosmopolitan hive of activity. Red squirrels hang upside on the baskets of nuts put out by the SWT while great tits and blue tits wait, not always patiently, for them to finish. The mixed woodland is full of song from the mellifluous willow warblers, yellowhammers, thrushes and blackbirds while otters silently go about their business. Swans swim seemingly effortlessly across the grey blue water chasing away busybody geese while cormorants spread their wings out to dry in the sun after their fishing trips; golden eye and eider dive for their meals.   A flash of blue and orange at the water's edge is often the only sign of that dapper little bird, the kingfisher. Ospreys are regulars to the loch, their nest built safely in the trees but just to prove that housing problems are not only for humans, their chosen spot has obviously been a good one for a pair of greylag geese found the nest a snug fit to have their own family, commandeering it just before the ospreys returned from Africa. The ospreys however have now proved they too can safely rear a family in this nest, their chick of last year having been spotted in far away Senegal. To watch these magnificent birds as they swoop to catch their unsuspecting meal from the dark waters or sit majestically in the high trees, enjoying the warm sunshine on their beautiful plumage is indeed an immense pleasure.

From the intimacy of Balgavies Loch, the Montrose Basin on the east coast is a much larger reserve covering over 750 hectares of salt marsh, reed beds, agricultural land, mudflats and both fresh and sea water. About a half hour's drive from Balgavies, it plays host to up to 65,000 pink-footed geese in winter as well as many more wintering waders and wildfowl. With this particular reserve it is best to have your own transport to cover the various hides around the basin. The Scottish Wildlife Visitor Centre is a good starting off point but for those who want to be on their own, at least for most of the time, a car or bike is essential. Before starting out to explore this area, it is worth finding out about the tides as it can make all the difference to what can be seen. At low tide, it is possible to see the remains of an old stone dyke about one mile in length running west to east across the centre of the basin. Called the Dronner's or possibly Drainer's Dyke, it was raised in 1670 in an attempt to reclaim the northern part of the basin. The project was abandoned however after the dyke was badly damaged in a storm.

There are three hides situated around the basin but for those who are happy simply walking close to the water at the basin's edge, the Lurgies is an excellent walk. According to the Scottish Wildlife Trust, this area of the reserve was a dock as far back as 1178 and was regularly used by flat-bottomed boats until the late 18th century. The land was reclaimed by building a wall now the sea wall and this path takes you along the top of it. It is a walk bursting with interest. Large beds of common reed and wet grassland lie on one side of the wall while the water on the other side provides a wonderful vista to the town of Montrose. Common seals often pop up to view your progress. If you are in good voice, seals enjoy joining in a good sing-song. Snipe, moorhen, red-breasted merganser, mallard, goosander, goldeneye to name but a few can also be spotted or heard along with yellowhammers and linnets. The River South Esk flowing from high up in the Angus glens enters the basin just above the Lurgies. At low tide, heron line up almost jostling for position to get the best fishing station by the river as it meanders around the basin. Male eiders croon to their mates. Sandpipers rush hither and thither, heads bobbing and curlews with their evocative call prod and poke the rich mud flats. Each hide provides a different view of this tidal basin. The smell of the sea is all around, beckoning not just to wildlife but humans as well. It is a fitting place to stop and enjoy this wonderful feast of nature.

Looking through the railway arches to Montrose Basin

Boats on Rescobie Loch

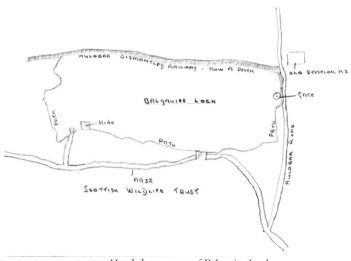

Hand-drawn map of Balgavies Loch

NOTES ON A SMALL COUNTRY GARDEN
WINTER

Many people hate December and January, the cold frosty morning travelling to work in the dark, coming home in the dark. The car not starting; having to navigate ice and snow. But as I have got older, I have learnt that to dismiss these months is to lose precious living time. I feel I get much more from life by embracing these months and what they have to offer. For me that is taking time to absorb the simplicity of that which surrounds me.

A geranium family wild flower 'Herb Robert' remains flowering in its sheltered position, albeit December. It was used for blood disorders in medieval times when it was known as 'Herba sancti ruperti'. A rain drop runs down a twig. It descends with quiet dignity landing in a stone water basin where the birds eagerly await the water before it freezes.

The morning began with a frozen mist but, looking at the wild gorse by the dry-stane dyke, it is covered in spider webs; threads of silk frozen in time made by the web-spider and unbelievably beautiful. The web-spider as a species is millions of years old and many legends surround it. One rather touching story is of the infant Jesus and family fleeing from Egypt. They hid in a cave and the web spider, noting this, went about weaving a web across the entrance. The Roman soldiers in pursuit, on seeing the web, formed the opinion that no one was inside the cave because the web was intact.

Echoes of ancient beliefs abound in this area of Angus. Standing stones, ley-lines, Roman roads, marching Roman cohorts, castles and monastic buildings, local history alludes to all of these, tantalising so.

This cottage is early 19th century around 1815/1820. It has been altered over the years but its walls are still three feet thick and it has a warmth and welcoming feel that makes you think that people have been happy here. No doubt its rooms were over-crowded; the toilet uncomfortably outside, a long walk to the local shop or to work in the village but its hearth would have been welcoming to friends and strangers; the garden full of vegetables with a pig sty at the bottom. As a child living here, one would have grown up knowing silence except for the sough of the wind as it moved through the trees. It is so difficult to find total quietness now for any length of time except when it snows. We have never been snowed in for long; a couple of days at most but that silence is unbelievable. Everything is hushed, cushioned and it gives you a taste of life without noise.

Snow alters the garden completely especially when the wind creates snow sculptures. It has an atmosphere all of its own. The footprints are there, then they are gone, hidden under a white blanket of crystals. When these have melted, it is as if we have never been.

It is time to pick some holly for house decorations. A fine old four foot thick holly hedge is just what is required at this time of year. The sparrows grumble but I laugh and tell them they can spare a few branches.

Some months ago, I gathered twenty or so Chinese lanterns (Physalis alkekengi) and put them in a large brown paper bag and into a dark cupboard thereby keeping their lovely orange colour. These wonderful fruit heads, although delicate, can be used for what I call 'fairy magic'. Pinhead light bulbs can be placed inside each fruit and each connected to the other. The string of lights are then connected to a transformer and switched on. String them on to shelves or the fireplace and pop off the house lights. It is just lovely to have something else from the garden in the middle of winter.

Although I don't have mistletoe in the garden, I always buy a few twigs of it. A lot of mystery surrounds this semi-parasitic plant. The Druids knew of it as did the Romans, Saxons and Vikings but it was the Christians that wove the story that mistletoe was once a tree in its own right. The timber of that tree had been used for the cross and for this vile deed, it could no longer be a majestic tree. It must now grow and depend on other trees as a parasite. I think I enjoy the other tradition better; the kissing bit!

Another year is nearly over and the garden rests. Being in the glen country, the garden is prepared for the worst but unfortunately the weather of late has changed and some of natures' plants and animals require more time to adapt. The loss of plants, shrubs and trees is always mourned but the loss of birds and animals is felt very keenly. There are eight blackbirds in the garden at the moment mingled with many other feathered friends including visiting bramblings. We will do our best to see them through.

Listening to the winter bird song, I remember reading this piece of Eastern philosophy and thinking how true:-

"A bird sang
Everyone listened
The sermon is preached
Said the Zen master."

166

Seed head in winter

BIBLIOGRAPHIES

Aberbrothock Illustrated – Notes by George Hay. Etchings by John Adam (Arbroath 1886)

Arbroath Herald

A History of Gardening in Scotland – E H M Cox 1935

Arbroath: The Royal Burgh of Romance – P Charles Carragher 1909

Britain's Countryside – Geoffrey Young 1991

Country Seasons – Philip Clucas 1978

East Coast Oil Town before 1700 – Duncan Fraser 1974

Focus on Fishing – Edna Hay and Bruce Walker

Longfellow's Book of Poems

Lunan Bay – The Scarborough of Scotland 1881

Montrose Review

Montrose Air Station Heritage Centre

Picturesque Forfarshire by Alan Reid

Scotland's Living Landscapes – Scottish Natural Heritage

Scotland's Gardens in old Times – Elizabeth S Haldane 1934

Seaweeds and Other Algae – C L Duddington

Tales of Lunan Bay – Colin Gibson

The Arbroath and Forfar Railway – Niall Ferguson

The Last of the Windjammers by Basil Lubbock – nautical publishers Brown, Son & Fergusson Ltd, Glasgow 1929

The Regality of Kirriemuir – Alan Reid 1909

The Red Castle of Lunan Bay by W Douglas Simpson MA.D.LITT.FSA Scot Paper Read 22 Feb. 1941

The New Statistical Account of Scotland Vol.10 1834-45

The Statistical Account of Scotland Vol.9 1791-99

The Third Statistical Account of Scotland – The County of Angus – Transport, Trade& Professions – Shipping

The Third Statistical Account of Scotland – The County of Angus 1977

The Flora of Arbroath and its Neighbourhood – the Arbroath Horticultural and Natural History Association 1882

The Grampian Quartet – Nan Shepherd 1996
The History of Arbroath by George Hay 1899
The Living Woodland – David Boag 1992
The Round 'O' – George Hay
Vintage Guide Newspapers – Arbroath Library
Vintage Herald Newspapers – Arbroath Library

REFERENCES

Abertay University, Dundee
William Gardiner – Botanist and Poet 1809-1852
Nan Shepherd – Nature Writer
City of Dundee Local History

LIST OF MAPS

OS 1:500 large scale town plan. Arbroath Sheet XLV1.11.24
    1859   *
OS 1:500 large scale town plan. Arbroath Sheet XLV1.15.04
    1859   *
Hand-drawn map of Balgavies Loch

*   Reproduced by kind permission of the Trustees of the
      National Library of Scotland

LIST OF PHOTOGRAPHS

Except where indicated, all photographs and hand-drawn map belong to the authors.

The scull, photographed in the story of the Fit o' the Toon, belongs to the authors.